PRETTY, PAID AND 40 POWERFUL DAYS TO EMPOWERING THE WOMAN WITHIN

PRESENTED BY JAKIA CHEATHAM MYLES

A PRETTY WOMEN HUSTLE NETWORK COLLABORATION

ISBN 978-0-578-86877-6

Being Pretty is the easy part. Getting paid while walking in your purpose? That's where the work comes in. You must dig up everything that has made you who you are and deal with it. When you truly walk in Purpose, your past can no longer stop you.

- Pretty Women Hustle Network

CONTENTS

How to use this book

First, let's talk about why we created this book in the first place. Flash Back to 2014. I felt as if I was on top of the world. Author of three books, founder of a ministry for Christian women worldwide, and the start of THE PRETTY WOMEN HUSTLE NETWORK. I was 18 years old and what was considered a Boss in my own right. At that time, I was booked and busy on a book tour and teaching women worldwide how to walk in their purpose. Sounds great, right?

A year later, I have lost everything. I became so focused on the world around me that following my dreams started to fall second place. I stopped posting, traveling, writing, etc. I gave up and lost myself. After that, I quickly decided that the boss in me was long gone. So, I searched for a job, and 9 to 5's became my new regular. I was desperate to fill a void that was honestly impossible to fill.

In the past five years, I have worked ridiculous jobs that have wrecked me emotionally and physically by working for people that frankly would not care if I were passionate about the job or not. I remember waking up one morning, saying, "This can't be life." Amid a pandemic, I gave myself 30 days to use all resources I had on hand to relaunch my hustle. I prayed and asked God to allow my hands to touch everything he has already created for me.

Sis, when I tell you that during those thirty days from April 2020 to May 2020, God stretched me in ways I could not even fathom. The countless nights of tears, losing access to our Instagram with more than 2K followers, losing access to our business email, and the list goes on. As God tried to elevate, the devil tried to navigate. But God endorsed our "level up" the whole way through.

I created this book to inspire and uplift the woman lying in her bed, ready to call it quits. It's for the young woman walking into her house after a long 8-hour shift, exhausted. This book is for the woman who has so many ideas but cannot figure out how to make those dreams realities.

This book was designed to take you through a 40-day journey of being stretched out of your comfort zone and thrown into your purpose. You will read stories of women from all walks of life to ignite the fire within you.

It is our hope that you use this book as a tool to inspire you to go after your dreams and aspirations. We hope this serves as a daily devotional that takes you into the stories of 20 women dedicated to living out their dreams.

We challenge you to set aside an hour daily to walk through the pages of this book, take notes and pray over your dreams and ideas. Please write down your goals and stick them everywhere and speak life over them.

Before you read each story, ask yourself these questions:

Where do I want to be in life?

What is my purpose?

What is stopping me from living the life I dream of?

How will I fix it?

What are the steps I need to take to walk in my purpose?

If you ask yourselves these questions before reading each chapter, I promise you this book will encourage the hustler within you. While this book is designed as a self-reflecting devotional, it can be used for group discussions among like-minded women.

As you read and reflect through this book, know that I am praying for you, and I pray that God will give you clarity and insight on the steps needed to live out your dreams. I pray your business reflects the time and work you put into being the best version of yourself for your business.

Day 1-2

Self Inflicted Pain
By Donita Covington

"The most delicate thing we have in life is a choice; those choices determine everything that shapes our lives; those choices become the blueprint to the legacy that we leave behind. When you feel the greatest joy or passion in your life, or when you feel like you have hit the deepest and lowest pits of hell, the feelings are as different as night and day, but each outcome came from something so pure and simple, a choice. A choice of whether we like it or not is self-inflicted pain often." - Donita Covington

Psalm 46:5 (KJV) "God is in the midst of her; she shall not be moved; God will help her when morning dawns."

Every morning that you wake up, God is giving you an opportunity to correct your yesterday. Every day you are blessed with another day, the day before is added to your life's blueprint, and only you can take advantage of any missed opportunity. As women, we carry loads and burdens that are often designed to break us, but through prayer, clarity, vision, and a purpose that we constantly manifest, we make each and every day our own unique footprint in the sand.

Philippians 4:6-8 (NLT)"Don't worry about anything, instead, pray about everything. Tell God what you need and thank Him for all He has done."

When life throws obstacles at us, why is it our first instinct to worry, then immediately after the worry, we start thinking about what WE need to do to come up with a resolution? Well, guess what? The problem or situation has never belonged to us to begin with, so our choice is all wrong. More often than not, when we choose to fix something that doesn't belong to us, we are self-inflicting whatever pain, joy, misery, or any other kind of emotion that comes from a choice. Instead of choosing, why don't we just immediately give it to God?

Proverbs 31:25 (NLT) "She is clothed with strength and dignity, and she laughs without fear of the future."

I have had and still have so many days that all I feel that I have in this world is pain, frustration, and a fake smile that I wear to keep people outside my darkness. We, as women, are often our own worst critics. We put so much out into the world, into our children, parents, siblings, friends, etc. Then, when we get nothing in return or get what we feel isn't comparable to what we give, we are hurt, angry, ashamed, desperate, and empty. We MUST learn to wear our choices, good or bad, the same way that we wear our faith when we have come through the storm. If we can have on the clothes of breakthrough, perseverance, ending storms, transitions, and anything else with so much pride when the light is shining on us, we need to wear hurt, loss, fear, shame, and loneliness the same way!

No matter what we are wearing, no matter the frustration, joy, anger, peace, brokenness, or wholeness we are in, wear it, own it, and know that nothing will last forever. This joy will eventually turn into pain. This heartache will be mended. Your income will multiply.

We must learn to wear anything that God gives us with our heads held high. Our future is uncertain to us, but God already knows the outcome. So, whatever space you are in, whatever clothes are gracing your back in this space and time, fear nothing! Keep your head high, and walk like you have everything already worked out because, through God, you do.

Sitting on my bathroom floor, I was in a place of abandonment. I was broken, scared, and felt that life simply had no place for me any longer. With a pill bottle in my hand and tears falling from my eyes, my hands shook, my mind raced, and my heart pounded in my chest as a sleeping beautiful newborn baby boy lay soundly asleep beside me.

I can just take this entire bottle of pills, and it would be over. My son deserves someone so much better than me. Someone who can guide him, pray over him, nurture him, breathe life into him. He doesn't need me. I am worthless, impulsive, alone, desperate, and broken. Love him how? I don't even know how to love myself.

All my life, I have seen things in black or white. I had no grey area. Middle ground didn't make sense to me. I couldn't comprehend how you could be on the fence about love, money, your life, kids, etc. At thirty-seven years old, I met a man who would alter my life in ways that I had no control over and felt that I couldn't pray or fight through.

When I say this man came into my life like a hurricane, that's exactly what he was like. I met him at an annual family day picnic in the park. When I initially saw him, all I saw was HIM. I didn't do what I normally do when it comes to men. I didn't take a deeper look. It was a quick glance of this tall, brown-skinned muscular man with the prettiest light brown eyes and the smile that could open heavens gates.

The butterflies in my stomach felt as though I was going to be sick. I had never felt anything like this in my life. However, I didn't meet him on this day. It would take several months for our paths to come together. I would say maybe six months after seeing that beautiful specimen of a man.

I had looked everywhere for him. Lord, I didn't know who I was looking for, but I was on social media searching my friends' pages, thinking he was possibly friends with someone I knew. I could never find a picture of him. No name, NOTHING! Then one day, one of my good friends called me and said, This guy named Issa wants you to call him. He is 34 years old, no kids, never married, doesn't smoke or drink, and he drives trucks."

I was like, "Say what now? Honey, where is he, and how does he know me?"

"Remember the pictures we took when we went to dinner for our girl's night? Well, I had posted them up, and he asked me who the dark-skinned girl was next to me."

By now, my head is spinning. So I said, "Okay. Give me his information," which she did.

I immediately went to the picture that she had tagged me in so I could see his comment, and God could have taken my soul at that very moment because the man I was looking at on Facebook was my mystery man from the family day at the park a few months back!

This couldn't be real. I had searched for him, and here he was. He found me. So, I rubbed my shaking hands together and texted him. Waiting for his reply felt like I was going to die. I seriously could not breathe. Next thing you know, the text message indicator on my phone goes off, and it was him!

After texting nonstop for almost two weeks, we decided to go out. Since he was coming home for a few days, we made plans. As our first date grew closer, I was so anxious but filled with joy. We talked and texted every day around the clock. I was just so captivated by him. He was so attentive, and his heart was so genuine. My normal investigative personality simply didn't exist.

I, normally being a person that only saw things in black or white, now had a grey area. He was my gray area. He was younger than me, but that was too bad; he was ambitious, had a good head on his shoulders, was childless, had a good-paying job, and was drama-free. He was heaven-sent.

Our first date finally came, and the rest was history. Every day that he was home, we were together, and when he wasn't home, we were on the phone. Growing up, I never had much happiness. I already had two kids from a previous marriage. They were the source of all my joy. Still, the older I got, the more I realized that I wanted a life outside of my kids. Taiyo Dionta Corlew was providing me with just that.

He had beautiful dark caramel skin, a muscular build, light brown eyes that were slightly slanted, and full beautiful lips; he was beautiful. The first time we made love, I swear it was something you only read about in books. He could tell that I was slightly nervous. I don't know why. It's not as if I were a virgin, but I felt like he was my first everything anytime I was with him.

Issa stood with his back against my bedroom door, just looking at me. It was like he could see through me. I almost felt slightly insecure, which caused me to bite down on my bottom lip as I stood there, unsure if I was about to pass out or if I was just intoxicated with lust.

He walked inside my personal space; he was so close to me that he could literally feel my heartbeat through my back. He leaned and gently kissed my neck, then lightly licked the same spot. My legs felt as though they would give out at any given moment. The entire night we were so in sync with each other, he was inhaling my every exhale, and I lost more and more of myself with every breath I took.

We dated exclusively for a few years. Things were good, but he was emotionally challenged. I realized that he associated sex with love, and I didn't understand it, but I was determined to try and date someone different from what I was used to. He was my gray area.

After a few years, I started to notice his distance. It started very subtly, which I attributed to his job. After all, he drove on a truck alone for days, weeks, and sometimes months at a time. Emotionally at this point, I was constantly coming out of my comfort zone while he stayed the same. I knew better, but this love was something I hadn't experienced, and I wanted to keep it.

Lying in bed one day, he asked me if I trusted him. I quickly said, "Of course." The next question that came out of his mouth almost knocked the air from my lungs. He asked if I would start a family with him. I was almost honored that he found me worthy of such a blessing. The way we made love that night defied the laws of gravity and attraction.

That night something woke me up out of a sound sleep; it was like something pulled me awake. I got up and went to the bathroom, washed my face, and sat on the side of the tub. I heard God's voice say, "No, this isn't for you." In the pits of my soul, I knew this statement was about having another baby, but I disregarded the words. I shook it off, climbed back in bed, and fell asleep.

A few months later, we found out that we were pregnant. If I could bottle up the joy that radiated from him and sell it, I would be a millionaire. Everything was perfect!

Almost four months into the pregnancy, I woke up one night with the worst cramping I had ever felt in my stomach. I was balled in a knot crying. As I got up to go to the bathroom, I felt something warm run down my legs. I looked down and saw blood.

At that moment, I lost all the air in my lungs. I called him screaming, and he immediately jumped at the sound of my cries. He could tell that something was wrong. We lost our first child that night on the bathroom floor in my bedroom. I was alone, in pain, and breaking.

However, little did I know, a change was coming, and the wave would be worse than a tsunami. For me, the pain lingered. My body felt different, but I had to be a mom. I had to work. I had to maintain friendships and family bonds. So, I pushed through as we women often do. However, it was different for Taiyo. Something in him broke, and I noticed that he shut me out of his pain.

When you love someone, your senses are so very keen when it comes to them. I started to notice things shift. I asked what we are often afraid to ask because of what the response could be. I asked him if he had cheated or been with anyone else. I don't know what made me ask him, but I did. I could feel it in his touch, but I needed him to confirm it, and he did. His response knocked the air out of my body; all I could do is cry! Then the tears were replaced by anger, and I needed to understand why. What had I done to be hurt this way?

After he told me he was sorry, he just looked at me with my kids, and it hurt because he felt like he was never going to have that. At that moment, I threw my pain to the side and immediately started to comfort and reassure him because that was more important, right? We continued to work on us, and we wanted to try again.

Six months later, we were pregnant again, and because of my age, we were able to find out very early that we were having TWINS! His excitement couldn't be matched. He started looking at me through those eyes of love again, which made me feel more like a real woman. I wasn't broken, after all. God saw fit to bless us again. This was meant to be.

Much like the last pregnancy, I talked to God and asked Him to watch over me and our babies and continue to bless us. And like the time before, I heard God's voice as clear as I could hear my own.

"NO." And like before, I ignored the sound of His voice and His warnings.

Two months after that prayer, with no prior warnings, no pain, no complications, I started cramping while I was out taking the same walk that I took every morning without an issue. The pain was so great I dropped to my knees, as my head rested on the concrete before me. My knees dug deep into the grass as I cried alone, praying to God that this was not happening again. I could feel the blood dripping from my body, and I knew that life was yet again slipping from my body, but why? What had I done wrong?

The conversation with Taiyo this time broke me worse than ever before, but unlike the first time with him, I didn't hear hurt in his tone. I heard frustration. I heard slight anger. I heard regret, even. And with the loss, he slipped further away from me than ever before.

This time there was no conversation about trying again. We kind of just kept moving, growing increasingly more distant, and I was so desperate to hold on. I needed to feel that love that he once gave me, but it wasn't there.

One day a month or so after we lost our twins, we were on the phone talking, and the conversation that we both had been feeling for a while now came up. He softly said, "I have been trying to find my way back to you, I just don't know… I don't know how to or if I even want to."

Those words pierced deeper than my soul, and no words could come from my mouth. I was simply at a complete loss of words. I couldn't even fight. I couldn't explain my heart. He was the center of me, but yet he was letting everything break.

With no hesitation or resistance, I hung up the phone. Of course, we still talked here and there, but it wasn't anything like before. I knew he was living his best life while my world was shattering. But I had a lot to look forward to. My daughter was about to graduate from high school. I was about to be an empty nester, and I was single again. Of course, this was God's destiny, right?

Two months before my daughter was scheduled to walk across the stage and receive her high school diploma, and one day before I was headed to Vegas for a girl strip, I went in to see my OBGYN for my annual appointment. As she checked my cervix, she looked at me and asked if I had been feeling okay and when I had had my last menstrual cycle. I slightly raised to look at her, wondering why she asked weird questions. She then asked the nurse to take some blood and had me to urinate in a cup. Although I was apprehensive, I did it. She told me to sit tight and to go ahead and get dressed.

Maybe twenty minutes later, she walked back into the room and told me that I was PREGNANT! *Say what? I can't be, how, why now? She had to be wrong.* But oh, she wasn't, so with so much shock in me, I dialed Taiyo's number and told him. There was no excitement in his voice. He just said, "Are you sure?" *Well, of course! She confirmed it.*

I didn't pray this time. I didn't ask God to cover me, the baby, nothing! Somewhere in my head, I had convinced myself that God was against me because every time I prayed for clarity and protection, I lost the baby. *Nope, not this time, God, I am going to just do this on my own.* Ridiculous thinking, right?

With every milestone of this pregnancy, I kept myself settled. I didn't do much. I didn't tell many people. I just wanted to hold this as close to me as possible. That way, if I experienced another loss, then it would be mine and mine alone for the most part. Taiyo was still distant, but through the distance, he managed to accommodate me. We took beautiful maternity pictures, had an amazing baby shower, and now that it was so close to our child's birth, he seemed a little better.

Our son was born the day before Taiyo's birthday. *What a better date.* He was standing proud in the delivery room, watching me feverishly, catering to me, holding me every step of the way. This felt like how we used to be, and once again, I prayed. I hadn't done that my entire pregnancy because God didn't want me happy, right? Not even ten hours after our baby was born, Taiyo laid in the hospital, taking pictures of himself to post on social media. *Ouch!* The same day, we were dismissed from the hospital, and he dropped us and immediately got on the road to go work.

A month went by, and I never heard from him unless I called. Two months went by, and nothing. Christmas and Thanksgiving came, and he was nowhere to be found. With every passing day, my spirit was breaking. *I feel so stupid. I have changed my entire life around to give this man the most amazing miracle, and he just disappeared, only calling sometimes and sending money.*

My older kids were away at college, so it was the baby and me. Time was passing me by. I was barely eating, not sleeping, just trapped in my own self-pity, my very own self inflicted pain because that is exactly what this was. Many times, God had warned me, but as most people feel, they know best. I kept fighting against his will until he finally gave me what I wanted, or was it what I wanted.

A part of me had to admit that deep down, I felt that the baby would bring Taiyo and me back together and give us back what we lost, but realizing I was wrong was the biggest slap in the face. It was humiliating. How was I now forty years old making dumb decisions? I should know better, right? The constant longing to belong, be needed, be loved, and be accepted had brought me to the edge of what felt like the end! So, I decided that I no longer wanted to fight. I no longer wanted to be all alone. I no longer wanted to fight for everything I had in life. I no longer wanted to look at my own skin and face in the mirror. Look what fighting had got me, NOTHING!

So I picked my beautiful son up, went into the bathroom, laid him on the floor beside me, and just looked down at him. He definitely deserved someone better. I wasn't a woman. I wasn't worthy of anything. All God put me on earth to do is make others happy while allowing me to smile in their background. I was tired of the background. For once, I wanted to be front and center. My death would be just that – my opportunity to be first, even if for just a minute. My older kids would be fine. I had given them the perfect blueprint to life. They had family that would see them through the pain, and my beautiful baby boy would be too young to even remember that me leaving him was my sacrifice for him to have someone better raise him, not a failure.

My head and heart ached with the same pulse. I couldn't take it. Life flashed before my eyes – pain, rejection, struggle, lack of support, unloved, alone, broken. Everything slapped me at once, and the tears were falling faster. I was shaking more, but I got the pill bottle open. Three pills down, and a jolt hit my body. It felt like an airplane hit me directly, but everything STOPPED!

I heard God. I felt his presence. I felt him wrap himself around me. No words were spoken from him this time. Being wrapped in God made me feel like I was living in a parallel universe. I could see clearly. I could see my life, my kids, my journey, my strength, my beauty, my desires, my failures, and my soul! When I was able to feel my surroundings again, I saw my phone in my hands, and the first person I texted was my best friend. For the first time ever, I reached out for help. God willed me back, and at that moment, I knew that I would be ok.

More often than not, we create our own heartbreak through the expectations that someone will finally see our hearts and the beauty that we hold. Just remember that no matter where you are in life, no matter the challenges you face or the fear you feel, your journey and your life has a purpose.

Listen to God. Those little instincts are him nudging us. Stop trying to create a life where things simply don't fit. Love yourself far more than you can ever love anyone else. No matter how dark your road gets or how lonely your journey is, it belongs to you. Don't be afraid to embrace it, especially during the storm of life. More often than not, the hardest truth is that a lot of the pain we go through and experience is self-inflicted pain. It's pain that we choose because we want to control the situation instead of trusting God who already has our journey planned out. We just have to allow our faith to be greater than our fear.

Pretty Women Reflect

- What lesson did you learn from the pain you chose?

____

____

- Pain changes us all. What are you doing differently to avoid making those choices again?

____

____

Day 3-4

The Mind of a Woman vs. Her Coin
By Latrina Caldwell

"Your value is set from the standards that you set for yourself" -Latrina Caldwell

The key is staying empowered through your praise. Having a solid higher power/universe, etc., will be helpful along your life journey. We are all on a personal journey towards becoming the best individual we can be.

It's time to unleash the power within yourself. Spend some time addressing your mental health so that you stay empowered through being the best you. Validate yourself on your insecurities through empowerment.

There are so many ways to stay empowered. Girlfriend, first, you must shift your mindset to understand that you are in control of you and your success. You must direct your focus to spend time working on you.

Think about it. We spend time on unbeneficial projects. Put your focus towards a beneficial project for your life. Every day, we have a new opportunity to be a better person than before, to utilize these precious moments we are blessed with. Value each day when you open your eyes.

Understand that you are a person first, and your coins don't define who you are. The coin defines your hard work in the hustle department, but it doesn't define who you are. It is never too late to get started with pursuing your dreams and completing a few goals. You set the tone for your coin. Having a healthy mental state can enhance the abundance of your coins.

Understand that you as a person are enough, but you create a brand to bring in the coins. Study yourself and what it will take to unleash the wealthy version of you. Stay encouraged by connecting with like-minded people and compliment other people on their success.

We must be ok with waiting until it's our turn to be in a leadership role. Your time will come. Utilize this time to create a plan of action for your future. Stay empowered by staying in control of yourself and your choices. You control the coin; the coin doe't control you.

Sometimes we must call a spade a spade. Most of us don't like to work. We like excuses, but guess what? Only hard work pays off. Nothing is given to us, so why not take advantage of being the best version of you. Enhance yourself, and then you can enhance your coins.

At this point, you should be at a stage of getting to know who you are and accepting who you are. If you are not aware of who you are, 's time to get to work. Study yourself, sit down, and grab a notebook. 's time to take notes. Make a list of pros and cons. List your goals and obstacles that may be preventing your goals. Life is all about choices. It is your choice to change. When you lack confidence in yourself, it will affect your hustle, coins, future, and stability.

Going forward, be the best version of yourself by empowering yourself through applying heavy self-care. Love on yourself during these unpredictable times we're in today. Read, network, and stay motivated.

To activate your hustle within, you will need to give up people, places, and things. Let your hustle speak for who you are. You have to do the work within yourself to stay focused. Just like we eat food every day, we have to feed our mental health food as well. Therefore, self-care is so important.

Think about it. We put so much strain on our minds and our bodies; we are overworked and mentally tired. We always have to figure it out. Some of us feel like we don't have anyone to turn or talk to. But that is false. There is help everywhere. The Bible says, if he seeks, he shall find.

At this point in your life, take a moment to get focused on you. When do we step up and put ourselves first? We have so many things against us as women. We have to work twice as hard to maintain anything. Make things easy so you can focus on securing the coin.

Just like you need life insurance, you need coin insurance. Take advantage of the world changing and change with it. Be ok with being able to sit down to focus on yourself. In order to be the best you and make the best coin, you have to be in a certain mindset. You will have to go through some things. If we live and pay attention, life will teach you everything you need to know.

Get in tune with you. If you are focused on yourself, securing the coin will come naturally. This is why we have to stay true to loving ourselves. Do the homework for your life. We all start somewhere.

I get so sick of people saying 's too late. It's never too late to be a better version of yourself. I can't stress this enough. This is your life; take control. Do what will make you happy and successful.

Do the research on you. Learn to evaluate yourself as a woman. Again, if you don't have goals, you need to sit down and write a few. Also, write out a plan of action. Light your own fire by staying empowered and motivated.

Encourage and motivate yourself. Stop waiting or expecting validation. Validate yourself. Start utilizing your resources available to you. Motivate yourself. Get up and dance. Cook and clean. Do something that requires you to shift your mindset at that moment. Stop settling for less.

Right now, you get an opportunity to take control of your life. You can set the tone. You can rebuild your foundation. Set the tone for your coin. Push yourself. You can have anything you want out of life. Hard work will always pay off.

Make a decision to take ownership and power in your life. Love and accept yourself, then apply the change. Anything is possible. Make conscious decisions over your life. In order to own and fully control your, you have to fully own and accept who you are.

You have to be the best woman you can be. Girlfriend, you have to represent. We are a tribe, a unity, a sisterhood, a family. Girlfriend, get your life and secure your coin. Remember, the two are separate but one and the same. See, the coin is an effect of your hard work, which means they go hand in hand. Girlfriend, I send positive energy toward your amazing journey toward self success through daily empowerment.

Pretty Woman Reflect

- Do you have a current budget?

____

____

- Is it beneficial, if not restructure it?

____

____

- Do you practice self-care?

____

____

- Self-care leads to self-success to secure your coins.

____

____

Day 5-6

Leaving My Nightmare
By Kendra McNutt

"When you are facing a choice that terrifies you, taking a giant leap of faith is exactly what you need to do." – Kendra McNutt

I met J through my college roommates. I was in my second year of studies in an environmental science course. I was a little over a year out of an extremely mentally and physically abusive relationship. I was struggling to find my worth and self-confidence. He adored me. I think a part of me always knew that we were not really meant to be together. However, he was really good to me at the start. He fixed my car, and he helped haul feed to my horse. We had so many mutual friends the fit was easy. It filled a longing at the time to have someone to look after me. I hadn't learned independence yet.

A few months after we started dating, his stepdad committed suicide. We moved in together shortly after that. The first few years were ok. We drank a lot together. He was always happiest with a drink in his hand. Two years into our relationship, I went to the doctor because I hadn't been feeling well and got a huge surprise when he told me I was pregnant. A few weeks after that, I had a miscarriage. We went on to have two beautiful daughters, got married, and bought a house.

At times it felt like our relationship was only held together by hopes and dreams. He was drinking heavily quite often and was emotionally distant. There was a day that he had left his phone in my truck and a message saying "Happy Birthday big guy, can't wait to see you" came through from an unknown number. When I asked who it was, he told me it was a friend of his that he'd grown up with that I knew, so I left it be even though it didn't sit right with my soul.

We'd always dreamed of a big family. Our relationship was rocky, but I was convinced we could make it work. He wanted a boy so badly, so we got pregnant again, hoping for a boy. At the 20-week ultrasound, the technician saw a possible issue with the baby. We were quickly referred to a specialist and soon found out that there were indeed several heart defects. The next few months were a blur of maintaining "normal" at home for the girls, balancing the frequent scans and fetal echos, discussing surgeries, finding a high-risk OB-GYN, seeing several cardiologists, and deciphering conflicting opinions.

My mental health was taking a beating. The divide between us grew even more. Our first son was born on a Wednesday evening after a scary and high-risk delivery. He was taken immediately to the NICU. I had complications and wasn't able to see him for several hours.

When we went the next afternoon to visit, he wasn't there. None of the nurses knew where he was. I was in full-blown panic mode. After a bit, it was sorted out, and we found out that he'd been airlifted to a different hospital for surgery. My doc wasn't going to discharge me, so I had to fight to be able to go to where he was.

My parents were on the way to the hospital with our girls so that they could meet their brother. We met them on the road for a quick bite to eat and some snuggles with my girls. We got to the hospital where my son was shortly after midnight. It was unfamiliar, and we had to park a long way away.

I clearly remember J walking quite fast, a long way in front of me, pausing only to tell me to " hurry up," and making fun of me for walking so slowly. There was no offer to get a wheelchair or to walk at my pace, though I'd just given birth around 30 hours earlier. The next day was spent meeting with doctors and the cardiac surgeon, enjoying baby cuddles, and settling in.

Early the next morning, we went to the NICU for one last snuggle before the baby went for surgery. After they wheeled him away to the OR, I was in tears, which was understandable as the rollercoaster of postpartum hormones were coupled with the terrifying experience of handing your baby over to the surgeon. J looked at me vehemently and said, "Just quit crying. This isn't about you."

At that moment, I knew our marriage would never be the same. A few weeks later, Dawson's cardiologist came in to chat. That day was different. The energy she carried into the room that day was heavy and apologetic.

She asked me to sit and said we needed to talk. I naively assumed it was about another surgery. I could see a team of people gathering in the hallway as my heart sunk. She apologized and said his screening had come back positive for Cystic Fibrosis, and the team of people were there to talk with me. My heart that was only starting to mend was torn apart again.

As I read through the literature they'd left, I realized it was likely our youngest daughter had it too. I could check off almost every symptom for her. Our world that was turned upside down was now in complete chaos. Although we had discussed 4 or 5 kids, I swore I was done.

It was getting close to Christmas when J came home from work one day, looked at me, and said I think you need to take a pregnancy test. If I could've shot daggers with my eyes, he'd be dead. How could it even be possible? There was no way! Well, I was about to find out that when God wants to bless us with a miracle, it doesn't matter our plans. Sure enough, I was pregnant.

I was angry, heartbroken, and excited all at the same moment. For a split second, I considered termination. I wasn't sure if I could handle any more. I went for an additional ultrasound at 34 weeks. The tech who started off chatty fell quiet; I could've heard a pin drop. She left the room, saying only that she'd be back in a minute. She came back in and said I could go.

Early the next morning, I got a phone call asking me to come to the city ASAP for another scan. That day I asked why God hated me so much, what I had done wrong in my life, and how I was going to manage.

I fell hard into a pretty rough patch in my life. My marriage was awful. I had three, soon-to-be four, kids that needed me. I had been a stay-at-home mom for several years. What in the world was I going to do, and how was I going to do it? I felt hopeless. I had a c-section early in the morning, along with the usual medical staff. There was a full NICU team in the OR.

J refused to come in with me. I'm super grateful my sister did so I didn't have to face it alone. He was whisked away after only getting to see him for a couple of seconds. It was hours before I was able to get up and go to the NICU to visit. By the time we were able to, his tiny head was covered in electrodes to watch for seizure activity. He was having roughly what would equate to 100-200 a day, so he was started on medication before he was even 24 hours old. As he continued to grow, the seizures kept returning. With the condition he has, it is common to perform a radical brain surgery to remove or disconnect the malformed half. I had to take him to the children's hospital, which is 2.5 hours one way, at least two times a month, and his brother at least once. He screamed a lot and didn't sleep well. I felt like a zombie.

J's drinking escalated, and he was regularly working away from home. When he was home, we fought. It was extremely rare that he'd offer to help with the kids, to let me sleep, or to go get groceries even, and the resentment I felt grew like wildfire. At a tender seven months old, I handed my baby over to a surgeon to remove part of his brain, then again at 15 months, to complete the resection of his entire left hemisphere. This is where I felt the final and fatal blow of any hope I had of salvaging my relationship.

It was late at night, four and a half weeks into a horrible recovery, four of them spent alone in the confines of a hospital room. D had developed an extremely rare blood infection and was teetering on the edge of needing to be transferred back to ICU. That day followed a long night of blood work, lumbar punctures, and several other tests, with 20 attempts to restart an IV, and many tears shed not only by me but by his sweet nurse too. When I called home looking for some support, my request was met with cold and callous words, "Put your big girl panties on and deal with it. What do you expect me to do?"

I fell into a deep dark hole. I felt alone. I loved my kids fiercely and knew at my core something needed to give way. There were so many nights I begged God not to let me wake up the next day or for there to be an "accident" that would just take us all. I felt the constant desperate ache of a soul ready to depart its body-bound existence. I didn't want to inflict pain on those left behind, but in my heart, I knew raising kids in that environment wasn't what they needed either. I couldn't let them grow up thinking this is what love was or the type of relationship they should have when they grew up either. The mental and emotional abuse had broken me down to a shell of what I had been.

One day I woke up, and something had shifted. I wasn't my old self. I was going to do it on my own! Part of me, ok, honestly 98% of me, knew it sounded crazy. I was worried about what everyone else would think, but with unclouded certainty, I knew it was exactly what I needed to do. I wasn't sure how, but I knew if God had given me that clarity, he would get me through. I wasn't given this crazy but amazing life for nothing!

It took me almost a year to get my head wrapped around how it was all going to work. I'd been a stay-at-home mom for the last five years. J had been out of town for work for several months, so I decided to load the kids up to visit him 4 hours away as a surprise. When he found out we were there, he was livid! He had a girl living with him, which I later found out was 1 out of 5 or 6 affairs he'd had over the years.

At the time, I couldn't understand why he wouldn't have been happy to see our kids, at least. The straw that broke the proverbial camel's back was when I asked for us to go to relationship counseling, and he said he wasn't paying any quack to tell him I was just a waste of his time. A few weeks later, on a sunny warm early October afternoon, he'd come home for a few days. I told him we needed to talk. Through tears and a trembling voice, I told him that he needed to stay gone. I couldn't allow my kids to think what we were modeling was love, and it would break my heart if they grew up and had relationships that mimicked what they saw between us.

The judgment I feared from others came swiftly and harshly, starting with his. He assured me that no one else would ever want me for various reasons. My family told me that I was crazy and selfish and needed to think about my kids. His family was sure it was me that was having an affair. In the midst of the storm, I held true to what I knew to be right in my heart. I knew my babies were looking up to me, and more than anything, they needed me to be okay. I learned their judgments came from a place of wanting to keep me in the boxes they had built, where they were comfortable with who and what I was, what they saw as "right." In their defense, they didn't know most of what was actually going on behind closed doors. Leaving was hard, so hard! But there's never been a day that I have looked back and wished that I would've done it differently.

I used to ask myself, "Who in their right mind leaves a marriage with four kids, and three of them are sick, with no job ?" I'll tell you who – a super badass woman who has seen her worth! It was time to dig in and figure out who I was again. I'd continually broken off pieces of myself to plug the holes of the sinking boat that I called marriage. I worked out, I ate better, and I learned that taking time to myself was not selfish.

I did a ton of soul searching to figure out what I was going to do with my life. A voice inside me kept whispering to me that I needed to help people, but I needed to honor myself first. I began to see the injustices in the world a little clearer. I slowly worked my way out of that deep dark pit of depression and hopelessness and started to build a life I truly love.

Eventually, the dark days became fewer and further apart. The tears that fell every time I had a few minutes alone dried up. The laughter that had left was starting to return. I could start to love myself again. I had been granted the gift of being able to see glimpses of my gifts, my light, and a sense of purpose that was bigger than the story I was living. I read a ton of self-help books and watched a million inspirational videos.

Day by day, a little at a time, I learned to love myself again. When all the kids were in school full time, I went back to school too. I needed something that would have a super flexible schedule so that I could still be the best mom I could be. I have always loved helping people feel better, so I started school to become a massage therapist. The two years of homework, weekend classes, and being a full-time mom were exhausting. The days would start at 6 a.m., and I'd fall into bed at around midnight. But I did it! And over the next few years, I built up a successful massage practice.

One by one, my schedule continued to fill, and the worries began to fall away. If I had the faith and courage to leave my nightmare of a marriage, I could do anything! It was a ton of long days and millions of tears, wondering if I was doing the right thing. Learning the grace of receiving judgment and growing from it has helped me in an unmeasurable way. Being told NO has become my guidepost to see if I'm in alignment with my core values. If I'm not, I reset my course, and if I am, I know it was not meant to be. Working for myself, I know I have the ability to help others in the ways I can serve them best without being bound by company policies and schedules.

One of the days that I was extremely down, I made a promise to myself that I would never quit learning and growing, that I would always help whoever I could, and that is what I live by. We're often told that we need to pick one thing and stick to it for life. I say that's a lie. We're meant to evolve, to find the pieces of us that we've given away to build others up, and in that retrieval, we change. As Tony Robbins says, "If you're not growing, you're dying" If you aren't living life authentically, how does it feel? When something isn't working for you and doesn't nourish your soul, it's not your calling.

I also believe sometimes we are drawn to something for a time because there is someone we are destined to meet or a lesson in where it's taken us. Never permanently tie yourself down to something that isn't filling your heart up.

I've now ventured out as a coach, specializing in building passionate and harmonious relationships as well as massaging part-time. There's still a lot I have to learn, but I dig into it daily so that I can be the best I possibly can. A few people in my life still like to criticize me, questioning how I can help others with relationships when I am currently single, but we wouldn't expect a surgeon to be the one under the knife, would we? It seems like those that find fault with us the most have the most to gain by keeping us small.

So, ladies, you need to let your light shine! Not only for yourself but also for your kids and the women ten steps behind you. YOU will be their guiding light, making their path easier! You are worth it! So worth it! Know in your soul who you are. Don't break off pieces of you to fill others up or fit inside their vision of what you should be. When you know in your heart how you can best serve others, chase that. Chase it with the reckless abandon of a child chasing a puppy!

Pretty Women Reflect

- What has been the most terrifying choice you've had to make?

____

____

- What scares you right now?

____

____

- How can you build your faith to know that everything will work out?

____

____

Day 7-8

Love Wrapped in Exhaustion
By Donita Covington

"Have you ever found yourself completely engulfed in life? Your mate, your job, your kids. All these things are everything you love, but you are wrapped so tightly in it that you can barely breathe. You have lost yourself in every aspect of your life. How can the very things we love make us so tired, drained, feeling worthless, or unworthy in these times? We are truly wrapped in the exhaustion of our love." – Donita Covington

Love: Love encompasses a range of strong and positive emotional and mental states, from the most sublime virtue or good habit, the deepest interpersonal affection, and to the simplest pleasure.

Exhaustion: Exhausted is spent, drained, and depleted. Though you might associate the word exhausted with people, it's a word that can be used to talk about anything that's depleted.

1 Corinthians 11:10 (NIV)

"Therefore, the woman ought to have a symbol of authority on her head, because of the angels."

Proverbs 31:25

"Strength and dignity are her clothing, And she smiles at the future."

Psalm 127:1-2 (NIV)

"Unless the Lord builds the house, the builders labor in vain. Unless the Lord watches over the city, the guards stand watch in vain. In vain, you rise early and stay up late, toiling for food to eat— for he grants sleep to those he loves."

Corinthians 13:13 (NIV)

"Three things will last forever--faith, hope, and love--and the greatest of these is love."

Someone walking in love does not seek to dishonor anyone and is not only after self-gain. Love is slow to anger and does not rejoice in anything evil. A person who works in love always looks for the truth and keeps no record of wrong.

God is the center of your universe. Nothing that we do is without him. However, more often than not, we try to write the story of our lives, often only looking to or trusting in God when we are tired or things go wrong on our journey. How can we still walk in our vision of the life we want but still have God be the center of our universe?

Love is such a profound word with meanings that vary from one person to the next. Love has been the most beautiful word and feeling that anyone has experienced, but it has also been the downfall of so many people and situations. Sometimes we sit and think about how this word can be such a gift and a curse.

I can think back to a relationship that I was in. This relationship in my mind was like the alpha and omega. Everything was about HIM! The day I met him was like any other day. Nothing felt unique or special, but when I bumped into him while I was in the grocery store getting fresh fruit, something in my gut screamed at me. Looking at him, I was like, *WOW. This man is beauty personified. Dark skin, full lips, high cheekbones, and low-cut hair with waves that looked like an ocean.*

From the time that we exchanged numbers, our interactions were so organic. Everything was natural and easy. But being a woman, we are natural nurturers, givers, lovers, and molders, so we take everything on full-fledged, giving one thousand percent of ourselves.

I can remember a time loving a man to the point that I prayed harder for him than I prayed for myself. I found myself constantly changing while he remained in his comfort zone. You ever love someone so much that you could feel every nerve in your body respond to him. I changed everything about myself. I didn't go out with friends because he wanted me home with him. I pushed myself to lose weight so that my body image was pleasing to him. I supported every dream and every desire, and as time passed on, I started to realize how drained I was.

I wasn't mentally feeding myself. I wasn't spiritually feeding myself. I was giving everything to him. I was so busy wrapping myself around him that I wasn't noticing the fact that he was starting to slip away. But once he started to turn cold, fear started to creep within me. *What am I doing wrong? Do I need to give more? Do I need to listen more? Am I not pretty enough? Is my body ugly? Does he hate my hair?* I blamed everything about myself to the point that I was hopeless, and at my lowest point, he used every ounce of love I had given against me.

He said, "You are always working. I never have time with you. You are always here. You never go out with your friends or give me space. You are suffocating me. Not to mention you don't turn me on anymore." BROKEN is all I felt. Those soul ties will leave you hopeless. Here I was realizing that I constantly chose a man that never chose me back. I lost my soul loving someone that didn't have a soul at all.

The pain inside me hurt so deeply that I started to resent the most beautiful parts of myself. Sometimes the pain we go through is transformative, and as uncomfortable as it is, that soul-aching pain has a purpose. I slowly started to figure myself out again. I started to feed ME, listen to ME, pray for ME. Bringing myself back into the real world required me to be selfish with myself, be comfortable with saying no and giving no explanation behind it, listening to the beat of my own heart, and following the footsteps from the journey inside my own soul.

Love had exhausted me, and that's because I was loving the wrong person. I wrapped myself in someone without knowing who I was and what I wanted or needed. I prayed through my pain, and at that moment, I realized that my pain had a purpose, and it was for me to discover ME!

The role of a woman never seems to stop. We truly wear every hat – mother, daughter, sister, friend, girlfriend, wife, teacher, supporter, fighter. You name it, and we do it. But why do we mask ourselves behind so many things? Why do we not get a portion of what we give?

Even when it comes to our jobs, we invest so much into Fortune 500 companies but are terrified to step out on our own and create the same wealth that we so willingly and freely give to corporate America. Fighting your way back from any type of exhausted state in life, regardless of what is causing it, should be the primary focus for us. If we give more of ourselves to others than we are giving ourselves, then we are hurting the core of who we are, and NOTHING and NO ONE is worth self-harm or self-pain. Never be ashamed for taking care of yourself, because if you don't, then who will?

Our life's journey should always be about prayer, focus, dedication, and self-love. If you are not feeding yourself and pouring into yourself, how can you pour into others? If God is not the Alpha and Omega of our lives, everything we are doing will always crumble. As women, we are powerful. We are profound. We are unique. We are spiritual. We are light. We are powerful. We are everything we fought for and were told we couldn't be. We are LOVE.

Pretty Women Reflect

- Why do some women not trust or hold on to hope and faith as much as they do love?

____

____

- Do we move like we have the authority to move? Meaning do we follow the rhythm within our souls? Do we act on that feeling deep in the pit of our guts? Or, do we move in accordance with the way life dictates us to move?

____

____

- How do you identify and show your strengths? Do you wear them like the finest of clothes, or do you throw on any old thing to show the world?

____

____

- How can we still walk in our vision of the life we want but still have God be the center of our universe?

____

____

- Love is one of the GREATEST emotions we can feel. It gives us extreme highs and extreme lows. Why do you think that this word can entangle so many complex emotions and outcomes in life? What has love created or given you in life?

____

____

Day 9-10

When I Get Over Me
By Precious Swain-Peaks

"Each day is another opportunity for me to be a better me than the day before." – Precious Swain-Peaks

When life gives us lemons, we have choices of what we want to do with them. Some will feel that they are at a dead end based on their knowing the lemon is bitter. Their inability to see the true potential in themselves causes them to feel limited because of the lemon's bitterness. I was my lemons.

See, I am the daughter of a heroin-addicted mother. My father was incarcerated. I had a strong determination to succeed and prove wrong those who said that I wouldn't. It is believed that the children of addicted or incarcerated parents are destined to fail, but that is a myth. I graduated from college with a 3.8 GPA. From an experience and educational level, I was ready for the career of my dreams. But emotionally, there was some work to be done. I was a walking volcano ready to spit fire at any given moment.

I decided that working for other people simply was not for me. The combination of my analytical personality and my degree allowed me to properly structure paperwork and crunch numbers in my sleep. So I decided to start a business.

This was short-lived because being pretty and smart was quickly overlooked because my mouth was wicked. See, because of my past, I hadn't developed basic social skills. Let me rephrase that. I was taught to be polite, mannerable, and extremely articulate, so I actually knew and understood basic social skills. My lack of empathy and the fact that I simply didn't care what anyone thought or felt is what prevailed. So when going into business, please remember that just because you own a business doesn't mean you don't need to have good customer service skills. It is important to not just know but to practice treating people with respect and kindness.

I moved to Florida, convinced a change of environment would help my situation, not yet realizing that what had to change was me. From one angle, it opened doors of opportunity because the market was wide open, but from another, I was introduced to someone I had never encountered before. Her name was racism. Too light for the black people and too dark for the white. It was like a trip to the dark side of wonderland.

See on the phone, that Cali accent and articulate dialect had the person on the other end convinced I was a Caucasian female. Neiman Marcus suit and Nine West pumps didn't mean a thing when they saw this caramel with cream skin come through the door. In most cases, having more education than the person that was doing the interview, there was always the great excuse of "we have already filled the position" or "this is an entry-level position. We were looking for someone with less experience." Some of you may have experienced similar situations. Don't let the closed-mindedness of others define your destiny. I began to realize at this time that everything happens for a reason.

While in college, my internship was done in the office of a record label. The blessing in that was, in addition to using my accounting skills, I also learned about the music business. I never expected it, but being versed in copyright law, performing rights organizations, royalties, and artist development were getting ready to change my life.

Over time, I met so many artists, producers, and engineers that worked from garages and spare bedrooms, spending money on studio time and cassette tapes not knowing what to do next. This was the rebirth of Imprecious Entertainment Services. This time my harsh demeanor didn't matter because my clients were rough around the edges as well. It actually turned out to be an asset because it wasn't easy being a woman in the entertainment industry. The statement "go hard or go home" was an understatement.

The casting couch was the way in for most women. Those who hadn't hit the couch had been an assistant, secretary, or something of that nature to some man in the business. So, upon meeting my clients and affiliates, I had to set the tone that I was not an assistant, and I was definitely not a sex toy.

Let's take a quick break in the story. We see a broken little girl. As a result of being forced to survive from a young age, she doesn't deal with people well. If we simply take the statistics written out by society, we assume that this little girl would end up like her parents or worse. Because of the anger and the natural instinct of fight or flight, we figure that her destiny would be to either find a man with money or work a dead-end job while living in low-income housing. Remember, "For I know את eth-the thoughts that I think toward you, says YAHUAH, thoughts of peace, and not of evil, to give you an expected end" (YIRMEYAHU (JEREMIAH) 29:11 את CEPHER). As we go through the rest of the story, watch Yahuah work.

So I stomped through business in my Dickies and Nike Cortez, proving that a woman can excel in the industry without compromising her integrity. The money was flowing, and I have mastered the skill of independent distribution. By 30 years old, I was on my second business, Groovin High Records. I had five artists, three producers, and a room full of DAT and ADAT machines. Never allow yourself to be put in a box. Remember that you are the driver in this car called life.

One by one, my clients start getting arrested. This was devastating for business, so I was forced to hop into the workforce. I walked into a call center for the first time in my life for an interview to be a customer service rep and walked out hired as a customer service manager. Favor. The training this company offered was world-class. I had now been trained how to speak softly with a smile while still not caring. My delivery was impeccable. After three years, I left to do accounting for a lawyer's office, where I trained as a paralegal. Through all of this, I still had my business going. I refused to give up, and though it was not making as much, it was still earning money.

Life happened yet again, and I moved to avoid being caught up in someone else's foolishness. I went back into customer service management, this time for a Fortune 500 company. Back in training, I earned a certification in customer service, marketing, and social media consulting. At that time, there was no Facebook or MySpace, just blackplanet.com, AOL chat, Yahoo chat, and some music sites. This training allowed me to take my business to the next level, offering services that others didn't even realize were an option.

Although I believed that the move would disrupt business, it catapulted me into a place of balance and growth. I had experienced first hand this scripture "But as for you, ye thought evil against me; but ELOHIYM meant it unto good, to bring to pass, as it is this day, to save much people alive" (BERE'SHIYTH (GENESIS) 50:20 את CEPHER). What the enemy had planned to use to derail my life was reversed by my Heavenly Father.

Now, I am not sure why it is presented like you can not have a job and a business but don't believe the hype. If you are going to build a business with a strong foundation, you will need to maintain life. Maintaining life requires money. So it is okay to have a job and build your business until it is strong enough to be profitable. It takes time management, budgeting, and being able to stick to a schedule so that you still have time for family and yourself.

Twenty years in, I have built three thriving businesses, raised seven gifted children, and never truly having found the correct way to love one another, I filed for a divorce. Here we go again—another snag. Because I allowed my husband to walk out front in the business for the last seven years while I focused on the kids, people didn't realize that I actually did the work. So I lose forty percent of my clientele base to my ex-husband. Life will happen, things will change, people will come, and people will go; you have to be determined that you will overcome these obstacles and keep pushing.

Some are going through similar trials. Some feel like they can't be a woman in business because they lack education, money, or the support of a man. Let me assure you that when you let go and let Yahuah lead the way, you will realize there is nothing you can't do.

The divorce was a setback financially and mentally, but emotionally I was fine. Once I disconnected from the final thing hindering my actual calling, things began to change, but this time it was different. Like fireworks on the Fourth of July, my life lit up in a beautiful array of colors.

Time alone gave me time to heal. I limited my business to 10 clients so I could focus on me. I dug deeper than I ever had before into scripture and building a stronger personal relationship with my Heavenly Father. I learned to understand myself. I learned that it was time for me to match all the educational credentials that I held. It was my destiny to succeed, but I had to get over me.

Today, I am a published author, Pastor of New Visions Ministries of Florida, Owner of Imprecious Entertainment Services, and still maintain the ten clients I have had for over ten years. I am the owner of Anointed For Prosperity Bookkeeping and More, which employs eight people and services hundreds of people each tax season. I am a partner in Swain Girl Media with my daughters and Peak Level Productions, LLC with my husband. When I let go of the anger, the pain, and the fear. When I stopped doing things to prove I could and began doing them because I liked to do them. When I stopped worrying about failing and realized that I couldn't actually fail as long as I tried, I absorbed positivity and grew beautifully.

So, here is some homework. Pray, then listen for the answer. Take your next steps in your business in faith, not fear or doubt. When you get into a rough patch, remember my story – a broken, damaged, hateful little girl whose faults the Creator looked past and gave her the strength to succeed.

Now gather up your lemons. Make a list of all the things you feel are hindering your growth or success in business. Remember, lemons can be made into lemonade, lemon meringue pie, lemon tarts, lemon cupcakes, and many other things. Find ways to overcome the obstacles on your list. Free resources, free courses, and other resources are just a google search away. You can do it.

Remember, "She seeks wool, and flax, and works willingly with her hands. She is like the merchants' ships; she brings her food from afar. She rises also while it is yet night, and gives meat to her household, and a portion to her maidens. She considers a field, and buys it: with the fruit of her hands she plants a vineyard. She girds her loins with strength, and strengthens her arms. She perceives that her merchandise is good: her candle goes not out by night" (MISHLEI (PROVERBS) 31:13-18 את CEPHER). We were designed to succeed in business and in our personal lives. Walk boldly into your destiny.

Pretty Women Reflect

- What is your biggest fear when it comes to starting your business?

____

____

- Did you know that making mistakes is the best lesson when developing a business?

____

____

- Do you realize that our Heavenly Father blessed us with minds to have and operate businesses?

____

____

- What's your next step?

____

____

Day 11-12

Be(Leave) In Yourself
By Adrienne Horn

"Doubting your dreams equates to labeling yourself a failure before you have given yourself a chance to succeed." – Adrienne Horn

Once you graduate from pharmacy school, what exactly do you plan on doing with your life?

The answer was most certainly not entrepreneurship. I wanted to be a pharmacist—nothing more, nothing less. After pledging a few organizations, working a full-time job, and studying for an average of five classes at a time, I was ready to jump into my career and discover the answer to that question one day at a time. Shifting from the classroom to my career was difficult, but being laid off, losing my six-figure salary, and becoming a business owner was even harder. School didn't prepare me for this, but I quickly expanded my thinking and transformed my worries into something beyond wonderful.

I was always fascinated by the power a pharmacist held. My mother, my uncle, and my aunt worked in the same field. I quickly learned I didn't have to stand behind a counter and speak to countless patients as I worked a 12-hour shift if I didn't want to. And I didn't want to. So, I made up my mind that I wasn't going to. I wouldn't fall into a career simply because someone told me it sounded like a good idea or that I would make a six-figure salary. I wanted something that would set me up to be "well off" and "successful." I was determined to wake up every morning and smile, knowing I chose a profession I absolutely loved and live a life I, at one time, could only dream of.

After being unable to obtain an internship or residency of any kind due to my having to take care of my mother, who had been diagnosed with breast cancer, I finally landed my first job in Miami Beach, FL, most commonly referred to as South Beach. One year after I had graduated with my doctorate, I was presented with this amazing opportunity to work for an up-and-coming compounding pharmacy that would soon be transitioning into the mail-order realm. I would be creating policies and procedures that would help the company do its part to improve patient care on a national scale. I was thrilled! I had done it. I had been offered a position as a working professional I was not qualified for and would be working in a place many people would kill for.

Life was starting to look up for me. I was well on my way to comfort, stability, and career advancement. I was 25 years old and reaching milestones that our society believes serve as indicators that a person was headed in the right direction and would eventually "make it." According to Forbes, less than 50% of U.S. workers feel that they have a good job. I had a great job and could thankfully say I was a part of the number of employees who were actually enjoying their careers.

During the Christmas season of 2016, I was very much happy with my position. In a little over a year, I had jumped from a five-figure salary to a six-figure salary, became the regional director for the corporate office, and managed to become a licensed pharmacist in FOURTEEN states, all while raising my one-year-old-daughter, Paris. Given the plight of our workforce during that time, I was beyond thankful to still be employed. Many companies had lost their best employees simply because they could no longer afford them, and here I was still receiving raises and bonuses.

When I entered the building the week before Christmas, I walked into my office and stared out of the window, looking toward the beach as I did every morning. The view was nothing short of breathtaking. When I looked down at the sidewalk, I saw so many walking in their designer outfits without a care in the world. I smiled because, in many ways, I felt like I was one of them. I was living my best life at a young age, and to me, that was a beautiful thing.

I walked to the Keurig and made a fresh cup of coffee. I ran through a list of things I needed to get done that week if I had any hope of having a great Christmas with Paris. Since I had missed her first birthday by 15 minutes (the flight was delayed) due to work, she was owed at least that. I picked up my pile of mail from the tray at the front desk and planned to go through all of it as soon as I checked my emails.

It was 8:00 a.m., and I already had issues requiring my attention. *This a problem that needs to be resolved BEFORE Christmas. We can't go into the new year this way. I will make sure to schedule a meeting AFTER the holiday season. They won't be focused, anyway. Ugh!*

Another denial? Why can't the licensing coordinator ever get these applications correct?

As I attempted to juggle the plans for work in my mind, I was halted by an email from the Chief Executive Officer of the company. It read:

Dear Dr. Horn,

Today is a sad and difficult day for all of us, but the time has come where we must address the present so that we can prepare for the future. While your dedication and work ethic has been exemplary, we will be closing our doors this year. Effective January 7, 2017, we will no longer need you to report to work.

Sincerest Regards,

S. C.

I must have read that email ten times before the tears started to fall. I was in complete disbelief. I had everything I could have ever wanted, and with three sentences, it was all taken away from me. I went above and beyond the call of duty every day with little to no complaints. I missed my daughter's birthday for a work emergency, for Christ's sake. And what did I get in return? A pink slip. I had officially been laid-off.

I was scared for my life. I had just moved into a brand-new townhouse and had a helpless one-year-old to take care of and a Christmas to plan. I had no one to turn to but God, and He just didn't seem to move fast enough. My racing heart had plummeted to the pit of my stomach and made me nauseous for what seemed like hours.

There was no Plan B. All I knew how to do was maneuver around office politics, secure my promotions, and help make money for the company. In an instant, I was mentally unhealthy. My stress level was through the roof, and I forced myself into a state of anxiety by constantly questioning whether or not depriving myself of sleep and working on the weekends had been enough. Was I enough?

In January 2017, the U.S. Bureau of Labor Statistics reported that 1,659,000 individuals had been laid off of their jobs, and I was one of them. The laughing and playing that was reserved for the weekend had been replaced with creating cover letters and revamping my résumé. By society's standards, I had come to a crossroads and selected the wrong path.

For as long as I can remember, I had this overwhelming desire to meet the approval of others. I pushed myself to be a straight-A student in high school, a leader in my community while in college, and an outstanding professional within my career. But that fire was gone now. I wasn't happy anymore because I had become the one thing I vowed never to be – a statistic. However, it didn't take me long to realize I had a choice to make. I could either continue doing what I was doing or branch out and try something new.

I had been laid-off for about two months and could not secure an interview with anyone. Sunday through Saturday, I spent more hours than I can count situated at a table with Paris in my lap looking for my next place of employment. The opportunities that were posted on various job boards seemed great, but I was not a great fit for their position. I felt the pressure of paying bills and taking care of my family as the funds I had dwindled to nothing.

I was desperate and figured that maybe it would just be best to go back to school to obtain my master's in public health. I knew I was competing with hundreds, if not thousands, of others who had just as many credentials as I had. However, I quickly removed that thought from my mind when it dawned on me that it would not be the immediate solution for a very emergent problem I had yet to resolve.

I will never forget one particular morning when I received an inbox message from a Facebook friend asking if I still did freelance editing. I had minored in English in college and used to edit essays and term papers to make additional money before I started working at a call center full-time. With the state I was in, there was no logical reason to tell him no. We needed the funds badly. I quoted him a price and proceeded to work on editing the poems for a poetry book he had planned to release that summer.

I finished the project that day, and he was extremely pleased with my work. To this day, I don't know what made me ask him if he minded referring me to others he knew that may need my services, but I did. The one trait that I have always possessed is ambition. I had come to a point in my life where I realized I had to channel that ambition into something creative if I was going to survive. After talking to my best friend that afternoon, I decided I would be an editor if I could not be a pharmacist.

I wish I could tell you that transitioning from being a pharmacist to becoming an entrepreneur was a seamless process, but it did not work out that way. I had to work small projects to get the funds I needed to hire the help I needed to help me make the money I needed to take care of me and my daughter. I continued to search for a job in the pharmacy industry, hoping that my résumé would be appealing to someone, but it did not happen that way. Life had pushed me off the diving board. I would either sink or swim. I chose to swim.

During my transformation, I was the most successful because I allowed myself to:

Be Bold – I had the courage to leave what was familiar and go after something that was so unlike anything I had ever done. Because of my decision, I have inspired others to follow me on my journey as an entrepreneur.

Be Teachable – I immediately surrounded myself with a community of individuals who had become entrepreneurs themselves. Listening to them allowed me to make fewer mistakes than I would have had I tried to do it on my own.

Be Consistent – I promoted myself and my services every single day without fail, even when I didn't feel like it. Your credentials do not equate to your potential. If you dedicate yourself to accomplishing your goals, you will triumph over every obstacle.

Be Creative – Don't be afraid to explore all of the gifts that you have been given. Each of us possesses something that can be beneficial to others. Once you discover how to convert your gifts into gains, the possibilities will be endless.

Be Faithful – Prepare yourself for the odd looks and awkward conversations with your friends and family. At the first sign of trouble, many will try to discourage you and tell you that it is a terrible idea. However, pray and stay the course. Great things always await those who are patient.

When I was laid off from my job, I lost my paycheck, my health insurance, and my 401K. It was sudden and completely unexpected. It would have been so much easier if I had been allowed to continue my desired path to career advancement. It was comfortable and familiar. However, if I had not experienced such a terrible time in my life, I may not have ever discovered all that I was capable of.

Being jobless gave me the push I needed to start my own editing company. Although it was initially a solution to a problem I knew I needed to solve quickly, I grew and learned so much as I built a new dream from scratch and watched it manifest in my reality. The process was not easy. I encountered a lot of opposition from some I thought would encourage me the most. However, once I took responsibility for myself, I went from being an insecure and jobless mother to a successful six-figure entrepreneur and speaker. You, too, are more than capable of achieving this same level of success, so don't you dare let anyone else tell you differently.

Pretty Women Reflect

- If you were laid off from your current place of employment today, what is the one talent you possess that could be transformed into a business of your own?

____

____

- Which three individuals you can look to for advice in creating your own business? Write those names down and seek their guidance so to keep you from making unavoidable mistakes.

____

____

Day 13-14

Ignite Your Fire Girl
By Jakia Cheatham – Myles

"Fuel your fire with faith!" – Jakia Cheatham-Myles

A part of being a powerful woman is that you must have some fire. You must be capable of igniting the fire within you, no matter the circumstances. To better understand how you ignite your fire, let's revisit what fire is. When under the right elements, such as oxygen, fire is a substance that will give off a dangerous amount of heat and a bright light. The fire can grow bigger when flammable energy is near it or is added to it. Putting big fires out can be very difficult. Sometimes even small fires are hard to put out depending on what started it.

The point of me giving that definition is to illustrate that a powerful woman is fire. When the right energy is bestowed on you, a blaze is set off in you. When you are around people who are flammable, your fire grows bigger. On the opposite side of that, if you surround yourself with people who can destroy your fire, it may start to dim. Life events can dim your fire, and some of those things we can't control. That is why it is important to add as much fuel and energy to your fire as you can. That way, when life throws you a difficult situation, you won't lose your shine.

Although I may make it sound like it's easy, I know for myself that it isn't. I grew up in what I like to call a twisted world. On the one hand, I was the granddaughter of one of the most well-known pastors in our city. If you were on the church scene, you knew of my family. Sounds glamourous, right? But when church was over and the cameras stopped rolling, I was faced with the real world.

I lived at home with my parents: my mom, who was the pastor's daughter, and my father, the ex-preacher turned drug addict. Growing up with a father who was incarcerated my whole childhood had a huge effect on me. My life was twisted. Everyone envied the glamour but didn't understand the hurt and pain that I had to endure.

For many years I had no fire, and my sole purpose was to dim the fire of others. I was miserable and wanted everyone to feel that way as well. God quickly took ahold of me. I was young when I was diagnosed with Scoliosis and had to undergo surgery. Everything changed so dramatically that year. I had to be schooled at home for medical reasons, so I missed out on the joys of high school memories.

I was told I would have to go to rehab to regain my ability to walk. Something that came so easy to others my age, I had to go to rehab to basically learn again. It hurt me, and even though it was scary, it was humbling for me. I decided I would not be weak anymore. I had to turn my sad situation around. I needed to get my fire back shining bright. I needed to be ignited. I didn't just want more for myself, but I needed more. I needed more fuel to get my fire back going. A powerful woman never loses her fire; it just gets a little dull and needs more fuel and heat.

Every morning I spoke life into myself. There was no more room for being defeated. I had to turn my situation around, and negativity wasn't going to get the job done. I realized that it was time for something better after years of pouting about my home life.

I started affirming the feelings I wanted to have about myself. I started speaking things into existence that I wanted to happen for myself. The changes and the attitude I wanted was claimed daily before any of it was actually happening. I started having faith. Even though it didn't look like things were changing for me, I believed that it would. That is the definition of faith. Faith and fire go hand in hand. Each time I went to therapy, I said these things:

- With God, all things are possible!
- With God, you can achieve your wildest dreams!
- With God, your visions are reachable!
- With God, you will succeed!
- With God, you will change lives!
- I am a PLANET SHAKER! (Yes, I was going to shake the Earth queen!)
- I am a GAME CHANGER!
- I am what the world has been waiting for.
- I can, I will, and I believe I will do great things.

Speaking life into yourself and saying daily affirmations are types of fuel that are free! You can add them to your fire at no cost. Eliminate negative phrases like "I can't" or "Never." You can do all things with God. Allow Him to intensify your fire. Surround yourself with others who will keep you "lit."

Every day I began to write. Yes, EVERY DAY! Literally! After writing every day, I published three books in no time. My bright and shining fire led me to create ministries and businesses on my own.

When I was a young girl, my goal was to be a lawyer, but I surpassed that. I am my own boss now. You may get frustrated because you didn't accomplish a goal. It wasn't because you couldn't, but it's because there is something better. A fire that is contained in a small area will eventually go out. But a fire that is surrounded by an open area with plenty of oxygen will spread and continue to shine.

Don't limit yourself to one small area because someone told you that you couldn't do something. Don't limit yourself because you are afraid to take chances. Don't limit yourself because you feel like there is no other option. That idea that you had in your head needs to get out for oxygen. The gift that you were given needs to get out for oxygen. Allow yourself to get out for oxygen. Let your fire spread. Take chances on yourself. The only way you can fail is by not trying.

In whatever trial or tribulation you face, fuel your fire with good energy and vibes from people who will ignite you and not let your fire go out. Some people are fire killers. Beware of those people who say, "You won't make any money doing that," or the infamous "if you say so." If you allow them to get too close, they will put your fire out.

A good way to beat a fire killer is to prove them wrong. Turn their negative energy into fuel for the fire within you. Surround yourself with people who will support you and push you. These people are fire benders. They grow your fire and put you in situations that will only help you grow.

Always think positively. Find a positive in every negative. Even if you start to feel down or depressed, remember it doesn't last long. You can feel sad, but don't give up. Use your anger and sadness for fuel to want and need more. Trust in God to bring you through it, and know that He is there every step of the way. Jeremiah 29:11 says His plans are not to harm you but for you to prosper. Therefore, anybody who tells you that you won't be something or can't do something is a LIAR because God already promised you prosperity.

I knew my fire was important and spreading when I began to touch the lives of other women who needed to be ignited. God will bless you so that you can bless others. Your light will draw others to you and pull some out of the darkness. Just imagine if I had given up. I could have caused those ladies to give up as well because I was supposed to be their guide through the darkness.

Even if you can't see it at the time, giving up affects more than just you. You are someone's light. You are someone's guide. Don't leave those people in the dark. You are pretty and powerful. Fuel your fire with faith, fire benders, and God. Ignite your fire, girl, and keep it lit!

Pretty Women Reflect

- Who around you ignites you to do more and want more out of life?

____

____

- What in your life needs a little more fire?

____

____

- What is stopping you from having the life you want?

____

____

Day 15-16

You Cannot Reach What Is In Front Of You Until You Let Go Of What Is Behind You

By Tiffany Brewster

"Find your purpose and prosper." – Tiffany Brewster

Anything that is not growing is dead, either spiritually, mentally, or physically. If you are on your growth path, you will lose some people along the way, and in most instances, you will lose yourself. We spend so much of our lives trying to be what others think of us that we lose sight of what our purpose in life is.

There is not a single person who has not faced trauma in their lives. The difference is some of us realized what our traumas are while others are fighting demons, trying to figure out if those triggers are because of past traumas. Our journey to self-growth is either going to make ourselves miserable or stronger. The amount of work is the same; it is up to you.

Growth is a scary path; it forces us to nakedly stare at our imperfections. Some of us find our purpose before we leave this earth, and some of us find our purpose when we are leaving this earth. Do not stunt your growth holding on to relationships that do not serve your purpose.

You cannot reach what is in front of you until you let go of what is behind. The only time you will have real change is when you are forced to step outside your comfort zone.

Growth is not an accomplishment; it is an everyday journey. For every day that we rise, we continue to work on the best versions of ourselves. To be aware is to know that our life is not our own. Everyone has a purpose. You can choose to walk in your truth and find your divine calling, or you can choose to be what others think of you. Life is all about choices, and the choices that we often make either leads us back to where we started or it takes us on an ever-changing journey.

Some of us do not want to admit that we are damaged. We are too afraid to do the work. We must be willing to let go of what was in order to grab onto what could be.

Our current mental health has a lot to do with what obstacles we either hold on to or overcome as children. Often, many issues we face in adulthood are the direct result of not healing our inner child.

Growing up, I was a very outspoken, fun, and loving child. Sexual trauma stole my voice, and I allowed my trauma to narrate my story. Though I knew what I had faced as a young girl, somehow, I was either too afraid or too stubborn to admit I was damaged. What I quickly realized was hurt people, hurt people. Obstacles we face in our childhood and do not fix often resurface in adulthood. Accountability is a big part of growth. A man with no accountability is a dangerous vessel, for he thinks growth is an accomplishment.

In my early twenties, I started this journey without counseling. I was a "strong black woman." I was going to wake up tomorrow and be a changed woman. Bam! Boy, was I wrong. Being strong stunted my growth. I needed to be vulnerable. I needed to sit in my truth and be still. At twenty-four, I started my journey to accountability. Yes, I had been molested as a young child, but it did not define me. It did not rewrite my story. It was only a paragraph in a chapter of my life. I could not continue to mask my hurt with anger. My abuser had gone on with his life while I was stuck on making a paragraph a book. When people do not know your story, they judge you by your title. Reality is complex, but perception is deadly! Walk-in your truth!

You must go through reconstruction.

Whatever your baggage is in life, unpack it, sort it out, and store it in its rightful place. Once you accept life for what it is and let go, though cliché, the sky is the limit, but first, you must identify your truth, hold yourself accountable, and reconstruct.

The most pivotal part of growth is establishing or building a foundation. Have you ever had a plant that had outgrown its soil or was no longer receiving nutrients from it, so you had to repot the entire plant? The first thing you did was change the pot, then replaced the old dirt.

Next, you gently placed the plant in the new soil and firmly packed it down. Use that as a tool in your reconstruction process. You must repot your life and change the old soil using the three **R**s:

- **R**elease any negative energy.
- **R**elinquish negative thoughts.
- **R**econnect with your inner self.

We can be our biggest enemies. The heaviest burdens we carry around are often in our heads. All it takes is a leap of faith. Failure is not the enemy. We often hold ourselves back, afraid of the unknown, yet immune to what we know is toxic because it is familiar. There is nothing more toxic than knowing a change is needed but choosing to be familiar. Stepping out on faith is one of the best decisions I ever made. A man is not a failure because he failed; it is because he did not try. Failure often leads us to our greatest accomplishments. Believing in yourself is key, even if your faith is the size of a mustard seed, for no faith at all will leave you thinking your dream is too big.

"When a man starts out to build a world, he starts first with himself." – Langston Hughes

In June of 2019, I lost my mother to breast cancer; it was one of the most difficult times of my life. However, it forced me to look at my own life. What are the things that I want to accomplish before I leave this earth? What mark will I leave once I have passed on? Honestly, there was not much that I had truly accomplished. Yes, I had graduated from college, bought my own home, and married the love of my life, but that was not enough. I was still empty. What I realized was those were societal goals placed in my head as a child.

Ever since I was a little girl, I wanted to be a writer. It has always been my first love. I remember writing a paper in the second grade, and my teacher was very adamant about me pursuing my dream to be an author. She often showcased my work and bragged to others about it. That was the first time that someone had spoken life into my dreams and gave me the courage and confidence to think that I could be a phenomenal writer.

After high school, I went to Columbia College Chicago for two years. Those were some of the happiest times of my life. Unfortunately, due to financial circumstances, I had to reroute my dreams of becoming a writer. When I lost my passion for writing, I lost myself. So, it is no surprise that when I started this journey to reconstruct myself, I fell back into the arms of writing.

I am no different from anyone of you. Change has no time or limit; it awaits your arrival and meets you with open arms. You must do the work; it is an ever-changing and scary journey, and you might fall back into your old antics in the beginning, but you must challenge yourself to push forward. Letting go of the past is essential.

When I began to let go of past pains and heartaches, I began to see the world through a different pair of eyes, and I was able to grab onto what I wanted to become. I quickly realized that there are no heights to reach; growth is about identifying your flaws, nurturing them, walking in your truth, and realizing that your purpose is bigger than you. Your past does not have to predict your future.

Find your light, seek self-awareness, and invest in your mental health. Whatever you seek to do in life, do it with and for passion. If you try to do something because everyone else is doing it, you will fail every time.

Often, we celebrate our accomplishments and hide our failures; we need to bask in both to recognize our areas of growth. There are no accomplishments without failures. Where there is pain, there is purpose. It is never too late in life to rebuild yourself. Only the dead are without opportunity. Find your purpose and prosper.

I thought at 36, now 37, it was too late to begin my journey. I was worried about how others would react to my vision. What if I fail? What if I am not ready? However, when your soul is ready, your path is paved. My vision is clearer than it has ever been. All I needed to do was let go of the baggage that was weighing me down, grab hold of my purpose, and decide that I no longer wanted to look back. I just needed to grab hold of what was in front of me and lunge forward.

Breaking cycles is not only about changing the way you think. It's about staying resilient during turbulent times, taking accountability for your actions, and stepping out on faith when fear is tugging at your shoulders. We have to be the change we want to see in the world in order to start a ripple effect.

I am no longer in denial about being damaged. You must reprogram your whole way of thinking in order to grow. You must work on yourself daily. Sometimes just acknowledging you need help is the first step in your journey.

The most important element to growth is letting go of the past and moving forward on your journey. You are never too old to start over, and there is no limit on the amount of times you can start over. If you fall back into your old ways, check yourself and move forward. A plan without a purpose is just a dream. Follow your heart, put purpose before pleasure and prosper. When we let go, we open the door for limitless opportunities to flood our lives.

When I let go of :

____

____

I will grab on to:

____

____

Release any negative energy. *List 15 negative emotions… **Example: Fear***	**R**elinquish negative thoughts. *Turn each negative emotion listed in the previous column into a positive action. **Example: step out on faith.***	**R**econnect with your inner self. *List ways to reconnect with your inner self. **Example: take accountability for your actions.***

Fifteen Affirmations To Fuel Your Journey

- Today I choose me.
- I am enough.
- My thoughts are powerful.
- I will no longer occupy my mind with thoughts that dim my journey.
- My flaws are not a crutch; they are a stepping stone.
- I am an innovator; my purpose will fuel others.
- I will peacefully walk away from relationships that no longer serve my purpose.
- Negative thoughts will no longer stunt my growth.
- I will hold myself accountable, for my life's work is never done.
- My happiness is my responsibility.
- My circle will reflect my inner self.
- My soul is ready; my road is paved.
- My fears will no longer control my actions.
- My capabilities are endless.
- My journey has just begun.

Pretty Women Reflect

- What affirmations do you use to fuel your journey?

____

____

- What negative experience will you release to become a better version of yourself?

____

____

Day 17-18

Grinding to Greatness
By Latrina Caldwell

"My lane wasn't available, so I created it" – Latrina Caldwell

Ladies, so many times, we seek validation from others when we were validated from birth. God validated every one of us when we were chosen for this life. A lot of people are not on this journey with you. Most people will not understand fully where you are headed in life. So please seek validation from within.

Every day is a new opportunity to start again. At some point, you need to own who and where you are in your life. When you accept it, change will apply. Grinding is an everyday process. It never ends. Hard work will pay off, but there is a certain level of discipline. You must be diligent with your life goals. If you don't go hard for ourself, who will?

By now, we're all aware that we're living in unpredictable times with COVID-19. During this pandemic, it is very hard to stay focused and empowered. But if you push through and stay persistent, you will see the other side of your hard work. If we do not continue to thrive, we will stunt our process of growth. Therefore, grinding is so important. It is simply performing repetitive actions until the goal is completed.

Most folks do not like to understand that we can be our own distractions. We tend to allow things to consume our minds that might detour our growth. You might get to a breaking point but remember why you are on this journey. Remember, you are on an assignment and a journey of self-awareness/self-satisfaction.

Keep going. Never give up on your goals. This is your time to grind and utilize the resources at hand, such as working from home. That will give you an opportunity to have more time to work on your goals.

The world has shifted. You are supposed to shift with it. Stop, take a moment, and do a self-evaluation of where you are in your life. Write out the pros and cons, do some research, and stay spiritually connected. These are a few simple steps you can do to start the grinding process. Grind is short term dedication and discipline so that you can relax on the results your hard work produced. You will have a daily fight within yourself to stay focused.

Having a strong spiritual connection, staying empowered is very important as well. Girl, feed your spirit so you can stay motivated. Empowerment is key to grinding in your everyday life. Empowerment can become the starting point for connecting with your 'potential power' and being able to access it fully in your everyday life.

Motivate yourself, girl! Get up, put some good music on, and cook your favorite meal. You have the power to change your atmosphere and take control of your life. We have to motivate ourselves; we have to encourage ourselves.

Also, utilize your resources, your friends, family, and community to gain support/empowerment. See, to get to greatness, it will take another level of discipline. You will almost have to have an out of body experience. You must step outside of yourself. Image yourself where you want to be in your life. Then create a goal plan and start the process to greatness. Being great simply means treating people the way you want to be treated and staying humble along this journey.

You must see the greatness within yourself right, look past the surface. Don't believe what others tell you; do the work and research for yourself. This is your life; it is only what you make of it.

You must stay persistent with yourself; you also must heal along the way. Greatness is an everlasting chase; you will encounter many distractions and obstacles along the way. Remember, every time you are one step closer to your goal, curveballs will appear, but you can prepare if you are aware.

Respecting the grind doesn't mean it will take you 10 years and 10,000 hours to become a master at whatever it is you're trying to do, but you have to put the work in. Take some time to satisfy your inner needs. This is your story; create your outline by putting in the work.

When you are in hustle mode, you jump on everything that comes across your path that might add to your success journey to greatness. Grind feels goal-oriented; it starts with a goal and ends with a goal.

Imagine yourself in your pure image of greatness, all because you decided to take the first step towards greatness for your life. Take the time/energy to invest in yourself. Put you first because if you don't, no one else will.

Start surrounding yourself with like-minded people. Remember, you can easily become a product of your environment; you have to protect your energy. If you want to own a business, start networking with business owners. If you want to lose weight, grab a reasonable gym membership (During COVID-19, look on YouTube for workout videos).

Make good use of your time. Start to put your energy in an effective place. If you feel that you need more of a support system, then you create one. Most of the time, you have to understand that entrepreneur is very lonely. Therefore self-love/care is crucial during the process towards self-made success.

You must stay prayed up. I realized late during my journey that I had to create my own table to eat from. I admired so much in another woman, but I had to find my place. Therefore, staying educated and connected to positive sources are detrimental during the grinding process. Staying motivated and empowered is also very important.

Motivate yourself. You and God are all you need first and foremost. Don't get me wrong; having a positive support system will increase/enhance your ability to succeed.

Keeping your mental health stable is also very important. Seek help if you need it. Help is available. Put you first and stop being afraid of stigmas. Do what is best for your growth. A true person in your life will motivate you to keep striving.

Never give up on yourself. You set the tone for how others view you. You never know who is watching you. Stay encouraged, girlfriend. Create your own lane; find a path that is designed for you. When it is for you, you will know without question.

Ladies, activate the hustle within you. Anything you do for 30 days has the potential to become a habit. Create good habits that will line up the hustle within you. Start writing goals in increments such as 3, 6, or 9 months. Journal your thoughts and steps along the way. Utilize your time management by creating a routine that will keep you on track towards greatness.

Life does not come with a rule book. You have to find your own way. You must create the vision for your life. Put the work in. Yes, you will continuously get tired, but take a mini-break for self-care, then back at it. Go harder than you than you did before. It is almost as if you gave yourself an energy boost. We must reboot our minds and bodies to stay on track.

I had to really look inside myself to soul seek and find out my purpose and my why. I also knew that because I have two amazing daughters that are watching me, I have to be the best I can be. I must learn about this amazing thing called life. I began to research. I have an extra layer of personal drive and resilience, plus I am diligent with my life goals.

I want more for myself. I do not want to settle for less. Through my spiritual connection, I learned who I am. I know what I have to offer, so I require the best. I also have to offer that. So, it is up to me to do the work. Every day is adding to my character and image. Stop taking things for granted and get serious about your hustle. Let your purpose kick in, then get busy. Get rid of the doubt, and go for it. Change with this new world we're about to embark on. Step outside of the box and activate your inner motivation/strength.

Also, understand that everyone's process is different, so don't get discouraged if things are not flowing as you expected. Just understand it's not my time yet. Accept it, just work harder because you know your time is coming. Set time aside by setting alarms if you have time. Take 5 or 10 minutes every day just to journal your goals and steps. This will help you stay motivated.

Girlfriend, be different, stand out. Follow your goals, create your own table of business/sisterhood. Join the Pretty Women Hustle network, get connected to some powerful empowerment groups. You must continue to motivate/encourage yourself. Grinding to greatness is a never-ending process.

Pretty Women Reflect

- Do you understand that you must be persistent and keep pushing?

____

____

- How have you experienced failure (In your opinion) and bounced back from it?

____

____

- List three goals within 6 months that you want to complete.

____

____

- Are you taking any steps to activate/achieve them?

____

____

Day 19-20

You Can and You Will
By Alrissa Jenkins

"Remember your power." – Alrissa Jenkins

Finding the hustle in you is the first step to achieving success in your life. Realize that it is your life. Do not compare your success to others. That is one of the biggest mistakes that we face in life. We often see others' success and just assume that we can master their goals and start comparing our business and life to theirs. Everyone has a different story and walk they are on, so walk at your own pace.

Your Past Does Not Define You

I now can say I am at a point where I am starting to see success and its benefits. It was not a process that happened overnight, and to be brutally honest, it was not a process that just happened within a year's time. My biggest issue was looking at the outside world. As I got older in life, I would throw pity parties for myself because I wasn't where the world wanted me to be. I would constantly speak negativity into my life. Out of fear, I would talk myself out of business ventures and opportunities in life.

Growing up, I always heard the verse from the Bible says that the power of life and death lies in the tongue. It was not until I was older that I realized how much the words you speak affect your life. My life was not moving the way I wanted it to move because I was not speaking life into myself. I was not feeding my mind. I was not nurturing my needs.

When I was 28, I was coming out of a bad relationship and promised myself it was time for a change. To do that, I had to shed some tears and have some conversations with myself to help me grow. Do not let anyone make you feel weak for crying. Crying is a sign of strength. Cry it out and find that inner strength in you that will make you continue.

Reality Check

Before starting a business or a new opportunity, you must dig within yourself. A reality check is needed. Be able to check yourself when you are wrong. Be able to accept your failures. Be able to move past it and ignite the hustle within you. It will not be easy, but it will be worth it. You always deserve the best you.

Speak life into yourself so that you will continue on the journey and purpose that God has set out for you. Manifest the goals that you want out of your life. Speak life into those goals as if you have already achieved them. Don't give up on what you are manifesting your life to be. Don't short yourself in your manifestation. Stand firm to what you are expecting to happen in your life. Keep your journal on you and speak life into the goals that you have written down. But also remember, you still have to work towards the goals that you are manifesting. Faith without work is dead.

Finding Your Why

I was not fulfilling my purpose in life because I never really sat down to think about why I wanted to be successful? Did I want to be successful to brag to others about the money in my account? Did I want to be successful to show my past relationships that I can be something? Did I want to be successful to show family members who doubted me that I could make it? My reasons why were all wrong. I had to dig deep and find my purpose.

I questioned both of my pregnancies. I had made up in my mind that life was just going to be downhill after having my two boys back to back. God had different plans for me, and the purpose of my kids was to show me I had a bigger purpose in life. I had a purpose in life that needed me to leave a legacy. My boys depending on me as their mom was more motivation than I could ever imagine. My purpose was not to brag to others. My purpose in life was to have a family that would be proud of me. I can truly say I make my family, husband, and kids proud, and that's enough for me to keep going.

Key Points To Remember In Life

- Remember that the road will not be easy. Remember, there will be sleepless nights. Igniting the hustle in you, you have to change your train of thought. Keep pushing towards your end goal.
- Each week set aside a set time where you meditate. Set

aside that time just for you. Get you a quiet space and write down your goals for the week. Keeping up with your goals, whether big or small, is pivotal to your success. Remember to count the small goals in your success as they matter too.

- Birds of a feather flock together. Having people in your corner who support your success and failures plays a big part in your success. Yes, it may be fun to have friends to go out with, to drink with, and to act up with, but that does not matter when you are trying to reach a goal in your life. You need a circle around you that will encourage you. You need a circle around you that will push you on the days you want to give up.
- Last but not least, as stated before, "You deserve the best you," I stand firm to that statement. The power lies within you. At all times, remember what you deserve. Take care of your mental health and your physical health. Embarking on the journey to find the hustle in you can be draining and leave you tired. Even if you have to set aside a day of the week that's strictly about you, do that. You do not want to fry your brain. Starting my businesses with my sisters, there would be times I would wake up in the middle of the night thinking of business ideas. Learn when to tell your body and mind that it's time for a time out.

Realize your worth. No matter how much time has passed, do not give up on what you set your goals on. Every season you have in your life will teach you valuable lessons; do not rush the season you are in. Rushing your seasons could lead you to miss the lesson that you need to activate your blessing. Reaching success granted me an opportunity I could never forget, and that's finding myself."

Pretty Women Reflect

- What did you take away from this chapter?

___

___

- What were the key points to remember?

___

___

- How important is it to find your why?

___

___

Day 21-22

Determined Day Dreamer
By Tia Reesey

"Awaken the inner goddess." – Tia Reesey

Determine

When reaching a goal, completing a task, or achieving a dream, you know it starts with a strong mindset of a powerful word called – determination.

Determination is strong in the human mindset. It keeps your mind focused on that task you are about to take, what you are about to do, how you are about to get there, the steps you'll need to get there, the timing and how long it will take to get there, and the work you'll have to put in to get there. Once it's all said and done, give yourself a beautiful reward at the end.

Daydreamer

Many of us, I'm sure, have been told we daydream a lot. A daydreamer has many different terms and meanings. Some examples are:

- a person who seems to drift off and get lost in their thoughts; it would take someone to call their name a few times to snap back to reality.
- a person who may be disinterested in a situation and their mind is somewhere.
- a person who has a dream wanting to do something for years and dreamed it for years and years but let fear, doubt, anxiety, and lack of support get in their way of taking a leap of faith.

Determined Daydreamer

In Spring 2016, I came up with this name. I always had determination. If it was something I wanted, I would do it and go after it by all means and wouldn't stop until I got there. I haven't stopped. That all goes back to those who doubted me from becoming a teen mom and completing high school after being told I wouldn't do it. Completing college when I struggled, I didn't think I'd make it out. I reached my goal in May 2016 by losing over 80lbs when I thought it was impossible to do on my own. It took lots of time, lots of focus, lots of work, blood, sweat, and tears, but I did it.

Since I was a child, I've been to that I daydream a lot, and I believe I do. That's where the daydreamer name came from. It also came from the quote I often see online: "Don't quit your DayDream."

I had so many dreams that started when I was 16. First was making a name for myself and becoming a writer. I wrote many times but threw it away because I felt it wouldn't take me anywhere or it was too dull. I often wrote about my life, traumatic childhood experiences, and life as a teen mom going up until adulthood. But writing was a hobby for me. I didn't think of it as a way to make money, but someday I hoped for it in the future.

After reading my daily morning devotion on May 31, 2016, I prayed and asked God to lead me. Times were difficult. I needed a change and to do something different in my life. I was just going to work and coming home. I was paying bills and had nothing to show for it. I wasn't happy. I wanted to do something else, even if I kept my job. But it would be hard to take on a second job being a single mom. I wanted to do something I would enjoy doing. I wanted to turn my passion into making money.

A week later, the woman I purchase my jewelry from had reached out to me and asked me if I wanted to join her team with Paparazzi Accessories, but I quickly turned down the invitation. I told her, " I am not good with sales. I don't have the time, the money, or the patience. I've tried Avon, Mary Kay, Itworks and failed it all". I knew there was a sign-up fee, a monthly fee for the website, and other fees, and I just couldn't afford to do it.

She assured me this was way different! "Only a one-time fee, no website fee, no other fees. Every woman loves jewelry, older and younger women, tall, short, fat, and thin. You will make your money back quickly, and you won't have to do anything. You'll make money in your sleep. You'll get a free website. People can shop from there."

After a convincing run down, I decided to give in and pay the last of what I had to sign on. I was skeptical. I felt I was wasting money again and would fail again for the fourth time. *What am I going to do with all this jewelry? Will I have anyone to sell to? Will anyone want to buy it? I'm not good with sales, and I don't know how to advertise and market? Why did I even sign up?* Those were the questions that played over and over in my mind. I became nervous and figured I would just try my best to sell everything I got in my starter kit, and then I wouldn't do it anymore. It may have taken me a while, but I would get back more than what I spent and would never again let anyone talk me into independent sales.

My team leader gave me tips and dives on what to do while waiting on my starter kit to arrive. One of the tips she gave was to post my website on Facebook. I took the advice, still sticking with my own plan. She also advised me to send an email or text message to all my friends, family, coworkers, and everyone I know and tell them I just started my paparazzi jewelry business and gave them the website. That was a great move.

Soon after, I had three people place orders on my website, where I was able to get a commission. I had gotten my starter kit, and with help from my team leader and a live event, I sold all my jewelry in two weeks! I not only made back all the money I spent and more, but I had fun doing it. I had a supportive team leader and teammates and a few customers, which later led to many. Some of those customers became my teammates four years later.

I am still having fun and loving it. I still am making money in my sleep with customers shopping from my website. I am now able to catch up on some bills. But my inner voice still tells me, "Don't quit your daydream!"

I always worked hard towards my dream and kept faith that one day it would become a reality. I can face my fear and bring my writing to life. In August 2019, my mentor announced she was doing a book collaboration. I took that as a perfect opportunity to finally bring my writing to life and finally have it published in a book, even if it's not my personal book.

I was still able to publish a story I wrote and dreamed of doing for the past 24 years. Always awaken the inner goddess in you. Never let fear or doubt hold you back from your dream.

Pretty Women Reflect

- What in your life are you determined to change or improve? Is there an area that lacks determination?

____

____

- Do you have a goal set, but it seems like you're stuck in daydream mode?

____

____

- What does being a determined daydreamer mean to you?

____

____

Day 23-24

Great Things Never Come From Comfort Zones
By Kristina Peck

"For success to be within your reach, you must start reaching for it." – Kristina Peck

How many times in your life have you REALLY wanted to do something but let fear, anxiety, and doubt get in your way? If you are anything like me, you have let self-doubt get in your way more than once.

Growing up, I was socially awkward, an outcast. I liked to be behind the scenes. I never wanted to be in the spotlight. Being in the limelight gave me anxiety, and I hated everything about it. I avoided it at all costs, even if being in the spotlight brought me amazing opportunities. I chose not to audition for school plays, All-County Chorus, sports, all sorts of things. I always thought that other people would not think I was good enough. The sad truth is, I did not think I was good enough. My negative mindset convinced me that everyone else would feel the same way about me.

So, if I am a self-doubter, why am I writing a motivational story? Great question. It seems like I would not be the type of person in this sort of book, doesn't it? Let me let you in a little secret: people change, and you can too.

It all started about four years ago. I was a newlywed, living on cloud nine. I was a new nurse graduate, my husband and I returned from a dream Disney honeymoon, and we had our own home. I was blissfully content.

I sat down at my computer desk to register for my nursing boards, and, per usual, I was distracted by the all-mighty Facebook. I started scrolling down my newsfeed and spotted an ad for AVON. I kind of knew what AVON was, but honestly, I did not think it was still a "thing." I clicked on the ad, and the next thing I know, I was paying $10 to signup and become a representative.

A few days went by, and I had completely forgotten I signed up to sell AVON until a package showed up at my door. It was a big kit full of products, brochures, samples. You get the idea. I planned on just using the products and never selling. Why? Because I could never do something like that. I could never be successful with AVON. How would I talk to people? My social anxiety was too much. I would not know how to promote my business. Heck, I did not know the first thing about having a business.

Something amazing happened a few days later. My neighbor, who owned a nail salon, wanted a brochure and offered to keep a few brochures at her salon. "Awesome!" I said to myself. Soon, I started to get more customers. I started to make money. I started to have fun.

But then I realized I could not just sell to people I know or know of. I would eventually have to get over myself and meet new people. Introduce myself and my business to people. I would have to learn to be okay with rejection.

I had connected with my AVON Mentors, and some way, somehow, they ignited a fire that had been lying still in my heart for years. I did not even know I had this passion, fight, and will inside me. I was excited. I wanted to be successful. I wanted to do this.

Within the first few months with AVON, I had built a team and received my first promotion to Bronze Ambassador. I collected a $500 bonus. I was connecting with people. I was calling leads. I was sharing my passion. I was a whole new person. I was unstoppable.

Four years later, I have a team of 91 representatives. I am a Silver Ambassador. I am running a successful business. I have won 3 Pinnacle Awards, reached the President's Club, and have made the top 100 list several times. It gets better, though. Now I am an Executive Director with the "Pretty Women Hustle Network." I am helping run a successful, established business. In late November 2020, I started my own marketing business, KP Marketing, which is quickly growing. I can't wait to continue sharing my success and knowledge with others.

A few years ago, I was too afraid to audition for a play where I would have only spoken three sentences, only to be never heard of again. Incredible how we can remold ourselves or retrain our minds, isn't it? Now all I think is, *why didn't I do this sooner?* I had this passion and fire in me all along, but I was too afraid to reveal it. I was essentially too afraid to be MYSELF. How terrible is that?

Anxiety and my mind tricked me into being a completely different version of myself for so many years. I suppressed my fire. I was convinced I was not meant to be or supposed to be successful. I was not supposed to be somebody, anybody. Now, I realize I was supposed to be somebody. I was supposed to be successful. I just let those negative thoughts rule my world.

So, girl, kick that self-doubt right out of your body! You CAN do this. Those voices in your head? They are not your enemy. They are your motivators. Use that self-doubt to ignite your fire. Step out of that comfort zone. How amazing would life be if you never had to say to yourself, "What if?" Just get out there and do it.

Leaving your comfort zone is scary, I know. BUT it is supposed to be! If you are scared or uncomfortable with a goal or dream, that is a GOOD thing. That means you are challenging yourself. I was scared the entire time I started my journey with AVON, but I knew it was a good thing. We need to challenge ourselves to grow. To be successful. To be a better version of ourselves.

I am not saying it will happen overnight, but you can light your fire just like I lit mine. Stop worrying about the naysayers, the pessimists. Forget about all that self-doubt. Sit down and seriously think about how incredible your life would be if you put all those things in a box and never opened it back up. Where would you be if you never let fear stop you?

Today is YOUR day. I believe in you 110%. I am willing to BET that you WILL be successful. All of those "dreams" you have? You can, and you will turn them into reality. Close that self-doubt chapter and open THIS chapter. From now on, you are writing a whole new book. You are in control. You call the shots. You can do anything.

Women are resilient. We were put on this earth to perform miracles. We grow a human inside of us and give birth, but we still think we are not good enough. Are you kidding me? We don't mind giving birth, but we are too afraid to better ourselves? We are seriously our own worst enemies. We hold ourselves back, and for what?

All too often, we let our self-doubt, anxiety, and fear control our lives. We let it drive for us. It pulls us away from a path full of self-fulfillment, success, money, and dreams. Why not be that person who takes the wheel and never looks back? That person who drives without turning around. That person can be you.

Sit down right now and make a goal list. Make a plan. Right now. Write down what you need to do to reach those goals. Do not tuck the list away in a dusty cabinet. Hang it on your wall. Tell your mama, daddy, friends, and co-workers all about your list. Let yourself be excited.

Do not hide behind your walls. Do not close yourself inside your comfort zone. Break down those walls. Turn your walls into a prospering garden. Water yourself with positivity and watch yourself grow into the successful woman you were always meant to be. Put all of your energy into believing yourself and watch how contagious it is. Watch how many people will believe in you all because you believe in yourself.

Being successful has its own meaning to each one of us. It could mean owning a business, going to college, or landing a dream job. Whether big or small, whatever your success story entails, always know that you can absolutely reach your dreams regardless of what anybody has ever told you. Your dreams are just sleeping and waiting for you to wake them up.

So, what are you doing? Are you still reading this chapter? Come on now! Get up, get out, and show everyone that newfound attitude of yours! Take that list and turn it into a reality. It is time to unleash the new and improved YOU—the woman you were always meant to be. I promise you it will be your new favorite accessory. Move over, Louis Vuitton! Unlike a Louis Vuitton, you better not put your new motivation away on a shelf. Carry it with you wherever you go. I bet your new self-confidence will get more compliments than your handbag does.

Pretty Women Reflect

- What is stopping you from being the best version of yourself?

____

____

- What can you do to become the best version of you?

____

____

Day 25-26

A Long Journey for A Victory
By Fida Abbott

"I'll never let anyone make me down. I have God who walks and guides me to the right places and does the right things." – Fida Abbott

In the nice tropical weather in the morning in early August 2002, I walked about fifteen minutes from my parents' house to the place where I would like to apply for an international driving license. I could go there by *becak,* but I used to walk. Besides being healthy, it also saved money.

I was very lucky. None of the customers were there. With my left hand holding the original and copied documents, my right hand knocked on the door. My smile bloomed after seeing who came to see me. He was one of the best friends of my aunt's husband. He worked at the driving license agency in north Surabaya. Knowing the person who would give me a service, I predicted the process would go smoothly.

After a short light chit-chat, I told him the purpose of my coming was to apply for an international driving license. He asked me where I would go. *Amerika Serikat* was my answer. Instantly, his face changed. He laughed, and in a trifle tone, he chimed in, "*Kampung Amerika?*" and laughed again. Listening to what I had just heard didn't bother me, even though it was very humiliating. For the people who live in a third-world country, going to the United States was impossible, except to those who are at least very rich or wealthy, have a duty from their company to go abroad, have a scholarship to study abroad, or have an invitation to visit the US from their families who have lived in the US. Also, at that time, one US dollar was worth more than twelve thousand IDR.

I smiled when he laughed. Looking at how he laughed, I had some thoughts in my mind: *How could my uncle have such a best friend like him? He laughed at me like seeing someone who wanted to go to a super-power country without any equipment. I didn't believe it was him. I even didn't think he would act like that. Did he know that I had an American fiancé and would go to the US to marry him? Did he know that my father was in the Navy and had been so popular because he was very smart? He was chosen to go to the Netherlands to study for thirteen months because the Indonesian Navy would buy a more modern warship? Did he know that my father had visited many countries during his duty in the Navy?*

Of course, he did not know! He knew me as a young lady who lived at her old grandma's house most of her life. He also didn't know I had temporarily just moved to my parents' house not far from that agency's office location and prepared for my moving to the US. Even more, he didn't know that I was a 32-year-old who looked much younger than my age. Many people thought I was in my early twenties, so it was understandable if he didn't respect me even though we were about ten years apart -- the same as my future husband. Or he probably thought I was a big, illogical dreamer!

Whatever he thought, I didn't care. I just needed him to process my application, so I handed all the needed documents with all their copies. But then he told me that I missed a copy of one document. He asked me to go several blocks from that place to make a copy while he waited for me and held all my copied documents. He said I could bring all my original documents with me.

It didn't take long. I came back in about less than fifteen minutes, but he wasn't there anymore. I tried to call with a loud voice to see if anyone was in that office. After trying several times, eventually, someone else came. He was very nice and friendly, but the problem was, he could not find my copied documents. He also told me that the first person I met didn't say anything when leaving the office to go to the driving center place.

I felt my blood rise. I didn't want him thinking that I was making up a story. In an angry voice I tried to hold, I asked him to try and find them again. While he was trying to find them, I felt my eyes almost wet. I tried as much as I could so that my tears would not fall. At the same time, I felt very humiliated by the first person. I thought that was why my eyes started to wet.

While my mind was planning what actions I needed to do if he could not find them, my concentration was dispersed. He found them in the drawer under the desk in front of me. He said he was very sorry and explained that he should not put them in that drawer, but the provided place with a note. I left that place with relief, but I could not hold my tears anymore. Tears of feeling humiliation changed to tears of great joy. Someone who was nice and friendly had helped to process my application.

Day to day, week to week, month to month, and year to year, I never told that to my husband. I had faith that if leaving my country to fly to the US to get married to my American fiancé was part of God's will, He would take care of me, and I would not perish. Even more, I never had a dream to go to the USA and live there. My goal was to get a job in Singapore and have a nice vacation in Australia. Those I could afford.

Because of my faith, I tried not to remember it anymore but focus on the future family I was going to have. I also remembered advice from one of my aunts when I was still a teenager. She said my future was in my hands and I should not let anyone destroy it. Deciding not to share that unpleasant experience with anyone, including my husband, I thought it would be a wise decision, and it helped me forget it. I could focus on my future, and that was true.

When Facebook started booming years ago, and Indonesia was the second-largest country where the people used it to connect with each other, I reconnected with my family and friends in Indonesia via Facebook, including my aunt whose husband has a best friend who works at that driving license agency. The old unpleasant memory drew me after over ten years, and I forgot it.

The good thing was I didn't feel any angry anymore. I wanted to know how he was or if he still worked at the same place, but all of those wishes just stayed in my mind. The other side of my mind wanted to meet him when we visit Indonesia someday, but then I thought it would be impossible. If we visited Indonesia someday, we would not stay more than two weeks and would also stay at the hotel and have less chance to meet him because he was not my best friend but my uncle's best friend. But I believe he had heard about me, my family, my books, or my works.

The young lady he once underestimated, now he would never do the same thing because she lives in the real USA country, not "*Kampung Amerika.*" She has a beautiful family, is an award-winning author in the USA for her books *Enthusiasm, A Novel Based on the Author's Own True Story* and *Exploring My Ideas*, has a special job as a foreign language (Indonesian) instructor for virtual classes serving the United States Air Force and holds a new intermittent position as a Language Consultant for Federal Government.

I believe I would not have a forgiving soul if I didn't have faith in God and trust that He would always walk with me in all the ways as I followed His guidance. The place where He wanted me to go would be where I planted a quality seed on the strong foundation (showing my faith) so that I could become a great blessing to my beautiful American family, others, and the new country I now reside in.

If you have someone or several persons who humiliated you or underestimated you, please write her/his name or their names along with reasons why he/she/they did that to you. Now, please write your own statement on how you prove that you are not what they think of you. Once you've done those things, forgive them! You will see the harvest you've sowed.

Pretty Women Reflect:

- As you finish reading this book, take a deep breath and ponder if there are any of your own stories you have similar to any stories written in this book. Write them down!

- A challenge for your good: If you are confident enough, you can share your story through your blog or social media to bless others.

Day 27-28

Say Goodbye to Fear and Doubt
By Jessica Kemp

"Look in the mirror and tell yourself to move out of your own way. Once you do that, you become unstoppable". – Jessica Kemp

With every choice we make, fear and doubt are right there. They are the unwelcomed guests in our heads that need a little push out the door. I constantly made excuses for why I couldn't become a children's author. In fact, I made so many of these excuses that I actually convinced myself that it was outside forces preventing me from chasing my dreams and not myself. It took a lot for me to get to a point where I realized that I was the only person standing in my way. I still may not have the best confidence yet, but I am insanely proud of taking that first step because now I am watching all my dreams come true.

As women, we are judged so harshly by society no matter what we choose to do. Staying single or getting married, having babies or not, working with babies, or staying home, everyone has an opinion on your life. You know whose opinion matters most? Yours! Stop letting the fear of what other people will think of you control your life.

There is this video that Will Smith released about his experience skydiving, and in it, he says, "God placed the best things in life on the other side of fear." No matter your beliefs, this quote still stands true because once we push past those fears and doubts, we are met with truly wonderful life experiences. We create our own fears and insecurities in our minds, and that is what holds us back from going after what we want.

Think of it this way. You wouldn't let someone treat you like a second choice, would you? Absolutely not! So why are you treating yourself that way? Stop making your dreams a second choice or a "what if" option. There might never be a sign or "right time" for you to make this change but when you take that first step, remember that you are now one step closer than you were the day before.

I thought I had to have everything figured out by the time I was 30, so I did everything possible to make sure I secured a "9-5 job." The problem with this was, I was sacrificing my own happiness because of my own fears about what others would think.

To all you lovely ladies reading this, let me share this one important fact with you: YOUR DREAMS HAVE NO AGE LIMIT, AND YOUR DREAMS HAVE NO TIME LIMIT.

When it comes to doing anything for myself, I am the queen of excuses, so believe me when I tell you that now is the time to get up and go after what you want. Yes, right now. I am not saying it will be an easy transition. Trust me, I am still trying to get through mine, but it is worth every struggle. There will come a day when you will say to yourself, "Why was I so scared? I wish I would have done this earlier."

It's impossible for us to have all the answers and know exactly what will happen, so a lot of us give up on our dreams. We let the fears and doubts take over, but you need to tell yourself that it stops now! Take back control; don't let fear determine what path your life takes.

I have a sign on my computer desk that reads "LOVE WHAT YOU DO," and it is my constant reminder that although I struggle at times, I'm working towards my dream of doing something that I love. Start with something visual. Print off a picture of your dream job and post it to your bathroom mirror. That way, every day you see it, you are motivated to push through. That right there is called step 1. Remember, no matter how small, all steps will lead you to success, but you have to keep moving. Your dreams are waiting for you on the other side of the finish line. They won't meet you halfway. You don't have to run. You can walk or even crawl but keep going.

Once you take that first step, you decide when to take the next one. There is no timeline. However, the longer you wait in between steps, the more likely you are to lose your motivation. If that happens, it's okay. Get up and try again. Push through that fear, push through that doubt, and go get that dream! Live the life that you want. Whether you are 20, 30, or even 50 years old, I believe in you. You got this! Life is way too short to go to work just to pay bills. We deserve to enjoy life. We are only given one so let's not waste it.

Now I know you must be thinking, who is this girl to sit there and tell me what to do. I hear you. I have read many articles and books where "people in my situation" are giving advice. Meanwhile, they grew up like a Kardashian. They never had to worry about daycare for kids, paying bills, etc. Well, that's not me! I'm telling you all this because I am literally going through these struggles as you read this.

I didn't go to school to be a writer. I didn't believe in myself, and I chose a different path. Now I'm starting from the very beginning, learning the skills on my own. I'm figuring out my work/mom balance, getting ready to move into a 2-bedroom apartment because we can't afford a house, struggling to find care for my daughter so I can work to help pay bills, and participating in all these writing projects on the side. Those are just a few of my roadblocks, and you may or may not be able to relate to them, but I think no matter what we are facing, it's about time we go after what we want.

I once heard someone say, "The longest relationship you will have is the one with yourself," and this is so true! Believe in yourself. You are capable of greatness.

Now, go over to the mirror and look at yourself. Look at that QUEEN! It won't be easy. There will always be obstacles, but don't you ever take that crown off! This is YOUR time to create magic. This is YOUR time to start showing yourself the respect you deserve. This is YOUR life. This is YOUR time. You can't fail if you keep trying, so don't stop until that dream is yours. Go get it!

Pretty Women Reflect

- What is stopping you from going after your dreams?

____

____

- Even if it takes you years to achieve it, what is one step you can do right now that will bring you closer to your dream?

____

____

Day 29-30

Breaking Through the Barriers
By Erin Montgomery

"I realized my dreams as an adult. As a mother. As a thirty-something-year-old woman. I realized my worth, my passion, and my purpose. Dreams don't stop just because you hit adulthood. You can and should grab hold of your dreams whether you're sixteen or forty." – Erin Montgomery

I am a single mom. For a while, I let that determine whether or not I could achieve something. As a mom, you are constantly filling the needs of your little ones, and it is both time-consuming and utterly rewarding. But when I became a single mom, I was consumed with the idea of providing for my children that I forgot about what I wanted in life. Why should I have to give up on my dreams simply because my "perfect" marriage didn't work out? Why is it that the mom is always the one putting herself and her aspirations on the back burner?

It was time to change that.

As a single mom, it was tough. I had to work ALL THE TIME. Money was tight, and sometimes it still is. I had to split myself between the home and the workplace. I was responsible for every drop off and pick up, every doctor's appointment or afternoon science fair. But I made it work. As moms, we all make it work. But something I noticed as I tried to reestablish myself in the career I left behind was that employers were quick to pass me over, regardless of my skill set or years of experience. I was met with a lot of disapproving looks or over sympathetic remarks, "Oh, you are a single mom? That must be so hard." or "Are you able to dedicate 40 hours a week for this role?" or "Who is going to take care of your children?"

Excuse me as I push my chair back, stand up, and shout: "AS A MOM, I AM THE MOST DEDICATED AND HARDWORKING EMPLOYEE!"

Just because I am a single mom doesn't make me less valuable as a person or as an employee. But I quickly realized that a "traditional" 9-5 position wouldn't cut it for me. And employers were, unfortunately, only looking for single people who would work overtime for free. And while I am willing and able to put in all the work, I also knew my worth.

I had dreams before I became a mom. I had a career. And while I chose to step back and raise my family, I shouldn't feel less valued because I decided to be there when my children needed me. I should be celebrated. I should be appreciated for my sacrifices. I should be held in the same regard as any other working person - regardless of my title as a mom. But that isn't how it always works out. And as a single mom, I needed to prove myself to those employers who said I couldn't do both. I needed to prove to society that being a single mom isn't a setback. It's a driving force to push forward. My kids don't hold me back. My kids didn't crush my dreams. If anything, my kids are the reason I made my dreams come true.

Now, this chapter isn't a pity party. It's not about how sad it is that single moms are quickly looked over for jobs. It's not about how hard single motherhood is, and let's be real; it is HARD. It's about what I did with my single motherhood. How I pushed myself to realize my dreams, make them happen, and create a life that my children and I are proud of.

★★★

During your childhood, you probably played a variety of different pretend games. Maybe one day, you were a vet and helped save the neighborhood dogs. Maybe you were a doctor and gave band-aids to all the kids on the block. Maybe you were an astronaut and built a spaceship. But as you grew up, you lost sight of those wild dreams. Where is that little girl who wanted to be a ballerina, a firefighter, a teacher? She is still inside of you. You just need to find her and let her out.

For as long as I can remember, I have always wanted to be a writer. I wrote a million different chapter books when I was younger. None of them made sense, and most were never finished. But I worked tirelessly to get all my ideas down onto the paper.

I went to college for journalism. I interned everywhere. I worked for free, and I got published. Soon I was making a living as a freelance writer. I was thrilled. I had become the writer I had always dreamed about becoming.

But life has this funny little way of throwing you complete curveballs out of left field. By 24, I was married, bought a house, and was seven months pregnant. Like most mothers, I quietly placed my writing career on the back burner and left it there for eight years.

Then, one hot summer day, I became a single mom to three children. I wallowed in self-pity for a while. I worked day and night as a bartender. I picked up every shift. I lost sleep. I lost out on time with my kids. But most importantly, I lost myself.

So what did I do about it?

I finally realized that my dreams were important.

I worked every day on my writing career. I started a magazine, went back to school, and enrolled in an editing certificate program. I finally realized that "the job" I had been searching for was right in front of me the whole time. I was a writer. This is what I was meant to do. This was my passion.

Once I found my passion and brought it back to life. I realized that my dreams should never have been placed on the back burner. I realized that the best way to show my children success was to show them that their mom followed her dreams. That no matter how difficult life got, how much sleep I gave up, or how many "no's" I heard, I pushed forward.

And now, I can proudly say that I made my own dreams come true. I am a published author, a writer, a freelance editor. I am the Editor-in-Chief of Flourish Magazine. I am the co-founder of the Single Parent Co., launching later this year. I am a single mom who made her dreams come true.

I encourage every woman, not just moms, to realize those dreams you had as a child. Find that passion you had as a child. Find the excitement in following your dreams. It's not easy. And I will not sugar coat it for you. I struggled in the beginning. And there are days where I still struggle. But it is possible. And it is the most rewarding feeling in the world.

If you feel like you are stuck in a rut, that you are just living to work and working to live, take a moment to reflect on what makes you happy, what drives you. Figure out where your passion is coming from. And turn that passion into your life's work.

No matter what stage of life you are in, whether you are married or not, whether you have children or not, it is never too late to realize your dreams. Even if those dreams become a small side hustle, it will be the most rewarding part of your day. Following your dreams and putting your ideas into motion - that feeling of I did it, is one of the most magical feelings, and I want every woman reading this to be able to feel it one day.

If you only take one thing away from this chapter, I want it to be this. You can achieve anything. You can be and do anything you set your mind to. We are constantly encouraging children to follow their dreams. We tell children they can be anything they want to be. But so can we. Just because we are adults doesn't mean our chance at our dreams goes away. Will it be a little harder to reach those dreams? Maybe. Will we have to work in a job we don't love while we build the future we want? Most definitely. But can we achieve those wild dreams we once had as children? Absolutely we can.

It's time for us to start believing in ourselves. I did. And I am proud of where I am today. It was not easy, and circumstances in my life may have made it a little harder, but I wouldn't have changed my path. That path, while sometimes broken and rocky, brought me to the place I am in today. And for that, I am grateful for every bump, every fork in the road, every sleepless night, and every tear I shed.

I realized my dreams as an adult. As a mother. As a thirty-something-year-old woman. If you placed your dreams on the back burner for the sake of your family. Now is the time to bring them forward. Because if not now, then when?

Pretty Women Reflect

- What are three "obstacles" that are standing in your way of achieving your goals?

____

____

- Write down 3 ways you can move past those obstacles.

____

____

- As a single mother, what is one thing you hope to teach your children about societal stereotypes as they grow up?

____

____

Day 31-32

Finding Strength in The Struggle
By Dr. Ketra Davenport – King

"For I know the plans I have for you," declares the LORD, "plans to prosper you and not to harm you, plans to give you hope and a future." Jeremiah 29:11 (NIV)

"I affirm I have the strength to overcome every struggle and walk by faith in each assignment that God has called me to do!"

"The struggle has no hold on the outcome" – Dr. Ketra Davenport – King

As women, we are faced with many obstacles in our lives every day. We are innately nurturing individuals, and our emotions drive who we are, what we do, and how we respond to fear and faith. We want to make all things right, not only for us but for those we love.

My morning walk is when I spend time meditating and seeking clarity from God. Today, the sky was ocean blue with cotton puff clouds, and the wind was blowing swiftly against my face with a cool breeze – it was the perfect morning for a walk. My spirit was wide open to hearing the voice of the Lord as we should be when seeking God's will for our lives and His strength, according to Ephesians 6:10-11 (NAB). *"Finally, draw your strength from the Lord and from his mighty power. Put on the armor of God so that you may be able to stand firm against the tactics of the devil."*

Reflecting on my life's journey over the years and how God has graciously bestowed His grace upon me, I realize that my strength came from knowing that God has been the wind pushing me forward during the good and bad times. Although we do not see the light at the end of the tunnel, we must be willing to have faith during the process to believe that God will be with us like the wind that touches our skin. Ladies, His spiritual presence is forever present even when we can not see Him.

One day about 15-years ago, my spiritual transformation began while sitting in my car, listening to Shekinah Glory's song, "Yes." The tears started to fall uncontrollably down my face. Life was hard. I was a single mother going to school, working full time, and struggling financially. It was overwhelming. In my weakest moment, God reminded me of His written promise in Jeremiah 29:11, "*For I know the thoughts that I think toward you, saith the Lord, thoughts of peace, and not of evil, to give you an expected end.*" This scripture has become my anchor to holding on to HOPE in Jesus Christ.

Jeremiah 29:11 is a declaration and promise that God already knows where we are in life, and He promised us an expected end. Be encouraged and find strength in the struggle because He knows the beginning and the end of our story. It is incredible to know that God knows the plans He has for each of us!

Do not give up, and do not throw in the towel. You are walking toward your purpose. God is amazing, and today is a new day to begin what you did not yesterday. Get up, Pretty Woman, and walk toward your destiny. Allow the wind to blow on you!

My encouragement for you is that you will "*find strength in the struggle.*" The wind is an illustrative example of the Holy Spirit as you walk in purpose (*i.e.*, entrepreneur, author, mother, wife, counselor, etc.). Understand that life challenges will come but keep your faith and trust God in the journey because He will be with you.

Pretty Woman, God is walking with you in every step you take. He is your strength. Believe that He will open doors that no man can shut. You are one of His chosen children, so keep walking and watch Him work!

God is faithful, Pretty Woman!

Pretty Women Reflect

- Have you taken the time to identify your struggles?

____

____

- What is holding your back and keeping you from walking toward your destiny?

____

____

Day 33-34

Every Pretty Face Needs a Side Hustle
By India White

"You can Overcome... ANYTHING!" – India White

When I think of the word *hustle*, I think of a drug dealer in the streets, making it happen for his pockets. A hustler doesn't have time for distractions; every move is highly calculated, and they are intentional with their purpose. This is how they become known and preferred over other hustlers.

Hustlers are great at building trust. They know how to follow through with scheduled appointments while planning consistent future appointments. Hustlers are likable and always know how to execute and deliver great services.

Additionally, hustlers know how to keep top secrets about their quality and what they offer to the world. They have a sense of suspicion about them that makes everyone curious. This is why people continue to come back for more and more. They have the IT Factor.

Now, don't get me wrong. I'm not trying to convince any of you to drop your 9-5 to go pick up a side hustling job that would put you at risk, such as a drug dealer. However, I AM giving you key nuggets that every lady will need to successfully operate a side hustle. Are you ready for it?

As a classy female hustler of your own side business, you must understand that your worth is priceless and that the world is waiting on your services! You must prepare for the best that's out there, no excuses. Choose to figure out what your side hustle will be and make it happen. Here are the main ingredients to being successful with your side hustle:

1. Know Your Purpose and Avoid Distractions

When you know your purpose, you are bound to achieve it and are determined to bring it to fruition no matter what is taking place. However, sometimes everyday life, meaning people and unexpected scenarios, can come up and distract you from achieving your goal. You may lose motivation and even give up for a moment. However, I want to encourage you never to quit until you have achieved your purpose.

I can remember being determined to have a graduate degree after I graduated from UF with a B.S. in math. However, what the world did not know was that at the time, I was in an abusive relationship in which I was forced to forfeit my scholarships and education. I got married and figured that I "made my bed and needed to lay in it." How many of you have heard this?

Well, that became the story of my life. I decided to settle in my mind while trying to do my best to cope with and accept my season of what I felt like was a mistake and a setback. I felt heavy and oppressed because I threw my dream away. I didn't know if I would ever have another chance at higher education because of the choices I made in my past. However, one day, I felt the Lord speak to me and tell me to apply for graduate school. I was pregnant with our second child by then and just couldn't see how I could be pregnant and go back to school. I obeyed anyway and was accepted at the University of Florida's College of Education within a week or so.

I went through a separation with my ex-husband and was forced to start over now as a single mother. Stigmatized and tight pocketed, I chose to remain optimistic and chase my dreams again! I was able to obtain my master's in Ed. Leadership at UF within a year and a half. Although I had to go into my promises and purposes with mistakes in hand, I owned my life choices, took full responsibility, and saw that my dream of obtaining an advanced degree would come true. And I want to encourage everyone reading this chapter by letting you know that it may be tough at first, but you too can obtain your dreams. So don't stop until you do!

2. Calculate Every Move!

To everything, there is a time and a purpose. You must choose to adapt and find out what your purpose is so you can achieve it. However, you must calculate every move. There is a scripture that says we must count the cost before taking on an assignment to ensure that we can achieve it. We have to make sure that the equation of our lives can be solved when we take on various tasks. Hence, calculation is key.

To effectively calculate, you must plan and have a deadline for when you would like to see things happen. Then, make sure it can be accomplished with your budget and your team. Whatever it takes to make it happen, go for it!

For example, I can remember when I had to decide to write a book and become an author. I contemplated writing a book for three years before I finally gave birth to my first book project. As a result, I was able to have success after consulting with mentors and loved ones. Now, I can say that I have written 30 books because I have effectively calculated what it takes to succeed as an author.

If you are trying to calculate your next move, don't be afraid to ask for help and reach out to others on your team or in your circle of influence to find out what to do. You'll be amazed at how eager some people will be to help you!

3. Write a Vision and Make it Plain!

There is a scripture that states, "Without a vision, the people perish." People are perishing left and right while remaining alive. They are throwing their lives away. Some of them don't even realize that the lack of vision is the main problem in their lives. However, once they obtain a vision, they are unbeatable!

Helen Keller was blind, but had a phenomenal vision and accomplished more than many of us who can see. Vision is a gift from God, and if someone lacks it, they must pray and ask for wisdom and guidance. Why? Because life is too precious to live multiple years, just to find out that you never fulfilled your purpose or that you came up short. Hence, vision is key.

I am an educational leader and have been for several years. How did this come about? Well, one day, I got alone with God and asked Him to tell me why I was majoring in math. It was always my heart's desire to become a stockbroker and to work for a Fortune 500 company. However, I heard a voice, and he told me, "I want you to teach." So, I was able to find peace and to take up a profession as a teacher. I do not regret ever following the will of God for my life. I can say now that, as a result, it has helped me grow as a leader. I've been blessed to fill some pretty neat roles as an Assistant Principal and National Education Consultant. This would not have happened, and I would not have been Teacher of the Year on two separate occasions and obtained my doctorate in education if I had not positioned myself to hear God's purpose for my life. As a result, my vision has continued to expand as an educational leader, and I'm so grateful for it!

4. Build Trust with Your Customers!

Business is all about trust. It is so hard to gain and so easy to lose. When trust is developed, the sky is the limit for you and your customer. Once someone trusts you as a reliable business partner, it will be hard for them to invest in others before first considering business with you. This is why it is so important to build trust.

Building trust simply happens when you are a woman of your word and back up what you say. Also, trust happens when people are convinced that you truly care for them, and not just their pocketbooks. When you can prove to them that you can solve their problems and help meet the need, then the business will flow.

I had a wonderful customer who bought most of my books because I was sincere and had their best interest at heart. I didn't even have to ask them to purchase them; they offered to! This is when trust is priceless, and that is where we all want to be. Figure out how to build trust with others and master your relationship building skills. Embrace emotional intelligence. When you are trusted with more clients, you must be willing to be more disciplined and trustworthy.

5. Know What Makes Your Brand Top Secret!

When I think of the best places to get a chicken sandwich, I will usually have Chic-Fil-A at the top of my list. Why? Because I know they are reliable, and I can find them in every state. Further, their brand has gained my trust over the years in various ways.

For one, my children LOVED Chic-Fil-A when they were growing up because they could play in the play area and eat an ice-cream cone after trading in their toy. Also, Chick-Fil-A was in one of the areas I went to study when I was working on my master's and my doctorate. The servers knew me by name and treated me with much care and hospitality. They even began to favor me when I was closer to achieving my degree because they enjoyed seeing me enter the building.

Long story short, not once did I mention the chicken that they served because the chicken was what I expected. What I did not expect and received was the extra service and classiness of their workers. This is what sets Chic-Fil-A apart from other restaurants. Seeing it is hard to build trust and to search out another restaurant, even if their chicken sandwich is amazing, my relational capital with Chic-Fil-A has been wonderfully built, and that's why I continue to go there.

Just like my example of Chic-Fil-A being a wonderful brand because of their customer service, people will be coming to you to find out what makes you awesome. My suggestion is...be YOU, and treat them AWESOME and watch everything else fall in place. Your brand will stand out for sure!

6. Keep Them Curious!

Many of us have heard the saying, "Curiosity killed the cat." Well, that's still true in our world today. People continue to watch scary movies or attend concerts because they are curious and want to know what will happen next. They want to see how a performer will end their show. Various things can strike someone's curiosity. We have to find out what that is and build ourselves so that people will be curious enough about our business that they will want to come back again and again.

As a motivational speaker, I always get asked to come back to speak because people want to know how I went from a homeless shelter to a college dorm overnight. They want to know how I went from walking the streets on Christmas day to Dr. White. They are mind-boggled because I am in the top 1% of at-risk that actually beats the odds. Senator Marco Rubio even commended me in his book and mentioned how I was an inspiration for America. But why?

This is why I continue to share my story with hundreds of thousands while raising multimillions of dollars in scholarships for students across the world. Every time I share my story, it will be different and will help that audience in a different way. I never get tired of telling my story, and I never get tired of fundraising for others. Over the past 18 years as a motivational speaker, I've not regretted it, and I am looking forward to more gigs in the future with phenomenal people!

7. Find Out What Your Customer Wants, Sell It, and Do it AGAIN!

I don't know about you, but when I go to the mall or shop online for a wallflower plugin from Bath & Body Works, it seems like I just can't get enough. I am loaded with guilt because I know I did WAY TOO MUCH shopping at that store…again. I usually try to discipline myself to purchase a handful of lotions and wallflowers but then…the $8 candles hit the selves, and I'm now in the red tape. Lol. I think we all can relate to that feeling of being stuck on our favorite retailer's page or in their store.

Well, guess what? Somebody out there is waiting for your services so they can feel the same way when they do business with you! You just have to find out what your business entails, what your brand is, and why your services are needed and wanted. Then, just make it happen!

Learn the voice and requests of your customer. Adjust your business if need be. Remember, keep your customer first, and they will keep your family first. It can take time to truly figure out your purpose and how to craft it, but once you do, then partner up with a phenomenal marketing team that will help you launch out like never before.

You may have to invest in yourself, and it will be worth every penny you spend. So I want to encourage you to find your worth in your brand and the value that you provide to your customers (like mentioned in the book, *The Challenger Sale*) and become a brand that they can no longer deny!

If you follow these steps, you will set yourself up for success! The best is yet to come for you as you develop your side hustle!

Let's connect! I'd love to speak with you as a motivational speaker, life coach and have you on my talk show, *Real Talk Show with Dr. India White*. You may reach me at India.White.123@gmail.com. Check out my website at www.india-white.com

Pretty Women Reflect

- What is the best way to begin finding your perfect side hustle?

____

____

- How can you develop the grit you need to sustain you when the hustle gets tough?

____

____

Day 35-36

Collaboration over Competition
By Shawntia Lee-Emilus

"My biggest competition is the reflection of myself." - Shawntia Lee-Emilus

Ever since I was a little kid, I could remember myself competing. Competing for attention with my sister, competing in school. Heck, I even played every sport possible so that I could compete and win. I had this burning desire and fire within to prove something to others, so they became my secret competitions. I participated in track, volleyball, and basketball. I remember the feeling of being in the moment and hearing my name called or being cheered for when my team was behind. Everyone knew and counted on me to turn the situation around.

It's only now that I realize everyone was waiting on me to show up because I was designed to achieve high results. I never knew people looked up to me for inspiration or desired to be in my presence. I was too busy looking at how I could crush the next goal or leave a lasting impression when I didn't even need to do all of those things. They already believed in me. I just didn't believe in myself.

Competition came so naturally that it became my way of living. Imagine how draining it was to constantly compete for acknowledgment when I already had it but hadn't taken the time to realize there was no need to overdo it. Anytime anyone would try and share their accomplishments or celebrate good things, I would always try and outdo them. It started with small things like breaking records, winning trophies, and playing sports, but then it turned into a livelong competition when I brought it into my relationships, friendships, and working relationships with my coworkers.

I thought this was an attractive feature, until one day I noticed my friends started disappearing. I thought, *awe, maybe they just got jealous because secretly I am outperforming them.* I would constantly hear my employers, friends, and even my husband ask, "Why do you always have to win?" It wasn't until this book and chapter that I realized I had developed this mechanism because I didn't want to look in the mirror. I didn't want to work on myself, so I exhausted myself by partaking in competitions that didn't even need my participation.

Where are you overcompensating for something because you are afraid to look in the mirror? Where have you wasted time and energy on something when you could have been devoting the same time and energy towards your purpose? This world is full of abundance, and wealth lies within. I cannot blame someone else for missing an opportunity or mission when I wasn't ready to receive it. I am here to tell you today, let go and collaborate. You have lived enough in isolation. It's time to unify and connect with others so that you may live your purpose.

This is for the woman who feels left out and overlooked. You are holding on to something that happened in your past. I am here as a witness to tell you that your fears, your doubts, your emotions, your spending habits, or lack thereof, are all you need to be worried about. I made some amazing relationships during my years, but imagine the ones I sabotaged all because I had decided "within" that I was not good enough and secretly competed with people, places, and things.

All of my blessings arrived when I started collaborating and building relationships. I am reaching success beyond my wildest dream. Hence, I am in a book collaboration. Now that in itself is funny. Today, I urge you to collaborate, open up, and receive all of God's blessings that are waiting for you.

Pretty Women Reflect

- Where are you self-sabotaging in your thoughts and actions?

____

____

- Who are you secretly competing with, and why do you feel the need to compete?

____

____

Day 37-38

Unleashing the Resiliency Within by Elevating Your Excellence
By Tiffani Teachey

"Walk in your purpose by being resilient, being your authentic self, and being persistent." – Tiffani Teachey

Turn your setbacks into comebacks. Resiliency is realizing that you are enough and being able to walk in your purpose. It is important to have a resilient mindset because our success is affected by how we view adversity and stress in life. We must bounce back from any setbacks and consider them as lessons learned to move on to an abundant life. I want to help women know that they are destined for greatness if they tap into a resilient mindset and attitude. Let's take a journey into how I went from a young woman with failures and doubts in life to becoming an unstoppable courageous woman who is living life like it's golden.

Tackling Life's Adversities, Crises, and Challenges

Resiliency is in everyone. It comes down to how well and how much you put your resiliency to use in your life. One can bounce back from difficult times in life through resilience. It is the mental strength gained through resilience that allows us to cope and adjust when dealing with hardship and stress. Resilient women will adhere to something and follow through with it. Resiliency is how one is affected and can adapt to changes, risk, adversity, and loss. Obstacles such as domestic violence, sexual harassment, and job discrimination are often what women have to face when it comes to being resilient.

It was shown that 70 percent of the women surveyed say they tend to be very resilient when they fail at something, and 45 percent say they don't regret having taken a risk even when they have failed because it has helped them learn, and they were still able to move ahead in their careers. These numbers are even higher (77 percent and 54 percent respectively) for women of color (KPMG Women's Leadership Study, 2019).

Resilience can start really early in life due to young girls having to deal with stressors caused by gender bias and expectations. Scientists found women were more resilient and lived longer overall, even during good times. When life expectancy increased, women still outlived men by an average of between six months and four years (UPI Science News, 2018). Successful aging can be tied to resilience and connected to the well-being of our physical and emotional health. One can live longer and healthier with the help of resilience.

Be Anxious for Nothing

I grew up with an entrepreneur father and teacher mother. As the first-born child with a younger brother, there were times that I was associated with having leadership attributes and being achievement-oriented. It was shown through many of the various accomplishments and involvement with being well rounded growing up. I was active in music, sports, and academics. My parents made sure that my brother and I valued education and made sure we took advantage of any scholastic programs growing up, such as the Math & Science Saturday Academy, which led to both of us majoring in engineering.

A Daddy's Love

As a daddy's girl, I always looked up to my father when I was growing up. He was a loving father, husband, entrepreneur, and veteran who instilled in his family the value of being family-oriented and the importance of love and hard work. He had lost his mother and father early when he was three years old from a car accident and was raised by his aunt and uncle with his other siblings. Therefore, he loved and cherished having his own family unit even more.

Having a good relationship with my father provided me with more confidence in myself and aided in my self-love. He was a proud father. Being self-employed, he had the flexibility to take me to school every morning alongside our frequent sit-down restaurant discussions, where he would remind me to be anxious for nothing (Philippians 4:6). It was something about the daddy-daughter bond that allowed me to see a hard-working father who loved his family.

Through all of my various accomplishments of graduating from high school to undergraduate and graduate degrees, my family was there. My dad always had his video camera, capturing every moment as a proud father with my mother and brother. To see the smile on his face with a sense of pride was a sight to see, especially as a daddy's girl.

It was when I turned 25 years old that I hosted a house warming on my birthday weekend. He was so proud to see his daughter become a homeowner and accomplish so much at a young age. My father began to get sick, and a stroke came on following the house warming. I was so worried. It was scary seeing my dad sick. It is something to see a parent become sick.

As he was getting the treatments to recover from the stroke, I would go home and check on him and encourage him to get better. He would look forward to seeing me and always be ready to show off his improvements and progress.

Within a couple of months, the family found out that my dad, although he was recovering from the stroke, was diagnosed with cancer that had begun spreading all over his body and had to start chemotherapy. I really couldn't grasp what was going on, and it was tough to see my father, who I looked up to be so strong and a leader of the family, become weak from this sickness. He had become at peace with life, at some point, and knew that he wasn't going to be with us too much longer.

When it was just my dad and me in the hospital room, he starred deeply and asked if I would be ok. I started to cry. In denial, I told him that he was going to make it. He told me to continue to be who I am and to make sure that the family unit remained connected no matter what and that he was proud of me.

Not too many days afterward, my mom called me while I was working to come to the hospital. The doctor said that my dad wasn't going to make it. I cried that whole drive to the hospital, and ironically the room was packed that I had to sit on the bed next to my dad. He was at peace to see his family with him as he passed away. I continue to cherish the moments, and it is tough at times, especially during the holidays, to think of the loss.

Growth and Reflection

I miss my father so much, but he encouraged me to keep impacting this world. He reminded me that our family namesakes are leaders. I was able to accomplish so much in my young adult life from working in the engineering field to homeownership and achieving various awards, continuing to give back in the community, and serving as a member of professional and service organizations such as the National Society of Black Engineers (NSBE), Delta Sigma Theta Sorority, Incorporated, and The Links, Incorporated.

I always have and continue to have the passion to pay it forward through service and becoming a youth mentor. It was a turning point in life when I was laid off after working in the industry for nine years due to the company project cuts. I felt at a loss when that happened, especially after I was so used to always achieving; it was a depressing moment dealing with unemployment. With the help of my faith in God and having the support of my family, friends, and sorority, I continually moved forward on this journey. Ultimately, God and my mom were my biggest supporters. I talked to them every day, and they helped me stay out of that depression mode.

I couldn't stay put in the job search sitting at home all day. Therefore, I made sure to volunteer to take my mind off of the current situation. The turning point for me was when I became politically engaged and served as the handler and scheduler on the campaign team for a mayor candidate. It was a great learning and humbling experience to help the first African-American female mayor of Charlotte and take part in history. Timing is everything as this opportunity happened during this time of reflection. Ten months after the layoff, I returned to my company with my service years and relocated to a new city. I thank God for allowing me to reflect, grow, and appreciate life more during this time.

Resilient Spirit

I went from a young woman with failures and doubts in life to becoming an unstoppable courageous woman who is living life like it's golden. I am a Sr. Mechanical Engineer, Science, Technology, Engineering, and Math (STEM) coach/advocate, professional speaker, bestselling author of the children's book, *What Can I Be? STEM Careers from A to Z*, and bestselling co-author of *Saving Lives While Fighting for Mine: Empowering Women to Win.*

As an engineer with more than sixteen years of experience, I have a passion for inspiring the next generation to engage in STEM careers. I remain politically engaged and encourage more to become registered to vote and get out and vote. I continue to be an active member of my various professional and service organizations. I enjoy traveling and being a youth mentor.

Steps to Being Resilient and Walking in Your Purpose

Be authentic – Walk the walk. Be your authentic self and journey from overcoming your obstacles to fulfilling your dreams. Your authenticity and attitude are functioned by resiliency and will allow you to have strong self-assurance and self-confidence.

Be consistent – Consistency is the key to becoming resilient in life. Figure out how you are going to use your gift to change the world. Take your passion and put it into action. Shape your own vision and be consistent.

Be persistent – Realize that you are enough and believe it. If you believe it, then you can achieve it. Your resilience and the choices you make will determine if you will thrive during difficult times in life. Be proactive instead of reactive when it comes to dealing with change. Shape your own vision.

Value your circle of influence – Surround yourself with positive people striving to be the best in life. Have supportive relationships and networks for problem-solving, support, and affirmation as you deal with life's journey of ups and downs, highs and lows. Many call these people your "Board of Directors."

We Are Conquers

I wanted to share my story of resilience and offer hope and inspiration to women facing adversity. I hope that I can help women by encouraging them to know that, if they tap into a resilient mindset and attitude, they are destined for greatness.

When my father passed away, it allowed me to look at life differently, and I decided to have the motto to live my life like it is golden. Life is too precious to allow anyone or anything to get in your way of having joy and peace in your life. Use these tests and trials in life to allow you to come out of it with a testimony of making it through. It is all about how you handle those difficult moments in life. Having a resilient mindset will guide you and keep you moving towards positivity despite all obstacles that come your way.

Pretty Women Reflect

- During challenging situations, do you keep a positive attitude?

____

____

- Who is your network of people that offers you support?

____

____

Day 39-40

Today Is
By Monica Leak

"Today is a new day filled with promises and possibilities." – Monica Leak

The words of Donald Lawrence's song entitled "Best Is Yet to Come'" is that spiritual, physical, emotional, mental boost needed in a time like this. With the outbreak of COVID-19 having us move from being out and about, traveling, socializing, hustling, jet setting, and being that boss lady to adjusting to the quarantine life, we all feel "some kind of way" about our days. You've moved from going to work in bumper to bumper traffic to working from home. You've moved from physical shopping to the use of delivery services. Those long in-person meetings have now become virtual with hopes that these can be more concise though that has not always been the case. Then, if you have children, it has made the days different as you navigate distance learning. This new math has got me stumped. The last day I remember is that Friday in March when we were sent home with a "See you in two weeks."

What we thought would be a quick turn around became a full-blown pandemic with people fighting in stores over Clorox wipes, toilet paper, and paper towels. I now have to look at my phone or computer to keep track of the days because they've all started to look the same. One day rolls into the next without much fanfare. It becomes just another day. Another day dawns, bringing about constant change. The bridge of the song challenges us to look at the day we've been given differently with the following words: "Today is the first day of the best days of your life. Today is the first day of the best days of your life. Today is the first day of the best days of your life." The repetition found in the bridge is like your mom coming to wake you up for school in the morning. It's that you've got to get up and do something mantra. It's that shake to wake you up from your slumber and put you in motion.

This is that hello, do you hear the message I'm trying to get to you? Today's message is full of promise and possibilities, that something better is on the horizon and that something great is coming. Yes, today is that day. How do we get to the fullness of what today is without limits or constraints? Let's start with a plan of action that will shift our current mindset and bring into reality what today is for our minds, bodies, and spirits.

You've probably heard it said many times: change your mind, change your life. The mind is where we gather, process, and sort information. It is the operating system of the brain. When our minds are unhealthy, our perception of people, places, and things in our lives can be off. We are unable to see things from a clear perspective.

Our minds are constantly being bombarded with things that we can't be without, or what would enhance our looks, or the laundry list of things according to experts that we "need to do" if we want to be successful. This can be a bunch of overwhelming crap if this is all we are taking in through our senses. All of the things we take in, see, hear, and do are fed through experiences, conversations, or media sources impact perception. It simply begins with the first thought.

What was your first thought: snooze, coffee, email check, social media scrolling, checking for text messages. Maybe your first thought was one of gratitude, just grateful to be in the land of the living. Maybe you hit the ground running with fresh faith and optimism. Proverbs 23:7 (NKJV) provides this nugget of wisdom: "For as he thinks in his heart, so is he." How do we begin to change our thinking? Believe it or not, you can take authority over your day. You can accomplish that through the power of your words. "Words kill, words give life; they're either poison or fruit—you choose" (Proverbs 18:21, Message).

What words will you choose to set your day? Here are a few affirmations to get you started: Today is a new day filled with promises and possibilities. Today I have clear vision and discernment. Today shines bright because of the light radiating from the inside. Today I am confident in my abilities and have a plan to reach my goals. Today I sow kindness and receive blessings. Today I have everything I need for my success.

Applying life-giving words is not limited to shifting our mindset but has an impact on physical well-being. So often, when experiencing any type of transition or trauma, our health takes a back seat. You're driving through fast food lines, binging on snack foods, and becoming lounge clothes wearing couch potatoes. Now I know there's nothing wrong with snacks in moderation, and Netflix and chill is a nice option to have, but too much of a good thing can result in what looks like college freshman fifteen. Your body is your temple. How you take care of your temple is how you will show up in the world. Amid a pandemic, protests around the nation, and just managing the day-to-day life issues, this is not the time to just let yourself go.

So with that same process of speaking and declaring over our minds, we now do so with our bodies. Today I see myself as the divine image of God. Today is the day I acknowledge my body as being wonderfully made. Today is the day I will choose wisely with whom I will share the treasure of my body. Today is the day I will detoxify my body of those things that are harmful. Today is the day I will hydrate and move in a way that serves to benefit my body. Today is the day I will commit to loving my body and will do unto it no harm.

Being a black woman, creative, brand expert, hard worker, mover, shaker, and problem-solver can be and is draining not only on the mind and body but also on the spirit. What is the pull on your soul as you watch protests in the streets, police in riot gear, and still try to wrap your mind around these reopening phases after months of quarantine? How do you capture the scattered and fragmented pieces of your spirit that scream for freedom and grieve for lives lost and yet long to rediscover joy? It is no easy task.

What you are experiencing didn't happen overnight, so the answers are not going to come that easily just because we're tired and fed up. So what is it going to take to reset and get our spirits in alignment? Do you spend hours in meditation or prayer? Do you virtually hop from religious experience to experience? Do you read all the books in the self-help, religious, or health and wellness sections of the public library or your local bookstore? Three keys to alignment: 1. Be still, 2. Listen, and 3. Speak.

If you're used to being in constant motion, being still can feel like a foreign concept or even a punishment. Yet, the advent of COVID-19 quickly made stillness a requirement. Psalms 46:10a gives us this wisdom, "Be still, and know that I am God!"

That be still is not a request or recommendation. It is a command, with you the subject, being understood. In stillness, you can focus and clear your mind of the negative energy that you may have encountered during your day. In the quietness, you can release what has weighed heavily on your spirit and be in the moment. Be still and know. Whatever your faith tradition, know that peace is coming, love is coming, hope is coming, joy is coming, and answers are coming in your stillness.

Being still allows you not only to center yourself but to hear what the Spirit has to say to you. What was the last thing you heard? What was the last instruction, direction, or wisdom you received? In this stillness, you can listen without interruption and unplug so you can receive the message the God of your understanding is trying to communicate to you. Pause and listen for it will be important for next moves, next steps, new ideas, and new concepts.

The last key I want to mention is that of speaking. Your voice is powerful and can build up or tear down; build bridges or disconnect, or bring life or cause harm. Too often, we have not recognized, owned, operated, or have misused that power and, as a result, have missed opportunities, damaged relationships, or found ourselves stuck in cycles of behavior. A lot of wisdom literature or sacred text talks about the power of speaking, so with that in mind, I share the following reference from Job 22:28 (KJV): "Thou shalt also decree a thing, and it shall be established unto thee: and the light shall shine upon thy ways."

Use your voice. Speak into existence what you want to happen. Speak change. Speak clarity of thought. Speak smooth transitions. Speak discernment and direction. Put a voice to your thoughts and ideas and release them. You will be surprised at how freeing this experience is. Today is the day I will speak life into my dreams. Today is the day I will speak joy into places of grief and pain. Today I will speak faith over my fears and leap. Today is the day I speak and embrace self-love and cast down self-doubt.

Today love is given and received. Today joy is found in the smallest moments or in the biggest celebrations. Today I have peace of mind during protests and the pandemic. Today I have perseverance through opposition, challenges, and obstacles. Today is filled with acts of kindness. Today is a good day. Today is faith in action. Today I am walking in humility. Today I am taking control of myself.

Choose this day to shift your approach in the moments, minutes, and hours of the day ahead, and I'm telling you from my own experience, you will see a difference. Today is whatever you want it to be. Speak it!

Pretty Women Reflect

- What will you say to yourself to set the tone for your day? Write a mantra or affirmation that you can post to remind yourself of the greatness of who you are and what your "Today Is" will be.

___

___

- What is one thing you can do this morning to shift the trajectory of your day, i.e., morning meditation, 15-20 minutes of exercise, journaling, trying a new lipstick, switching up your style, etc.?

___

___

Co-Authors

Donita Covington

Co-Author

Donita Covington is a mother to three kids whom she has tirelessly devoted her life to giving them opportunities that she didn't have growing up. Born in Nashville, TN she has moved around a lot growing up, which helped her to adjust to almost any person or situation she encounters. She is an only child, which served as a catalyst for her passion of writing and self-expression. Growing up with no strings or family ties, her inner most thoughts and feelings are often the things that hit her daily. Writing and communication is Donita's first love, but she also enjoys spending time with family and friends, along with traveling.

Latrina Caldwell

Co-Author

Latrina Caldwell is a Certified Life Coach and Psychotherapist Practitioner focused on mental health. She is a serial entrepreneur and Founder / CEO of Choose 2 Change Coaching and Consulting. Latrina also is the author of "I am HER" currently available on Amazon and "The Inside Job" coming very soon.

Latrina has completed formal education in Human Services and served for over a decade in Social Services. Latrina wears many hats as a Magazine Columnist, City Commissioner, Model, Motivational Speaker, Blogger and Actress. Her areas of expertise in coaching are specific to healing, relationships, family, careers, finance, self-love, self-care, self-confidence, self-esteem, domestic violence, homelessness and empowerment. She has experience working with adolescents and adults from various diverse cultural backgrounds.

As a survivor of domestic violence, Latrina understands the feeling of helplessness that comes from trauma and that the journey to independence is not easy. She wants to give back to the communities that she loves as a beacon of comfort, healing, empowerment, growth and understanding.

Her approach to coaching is grounded in the values of empowerment, hard work, personal commitment and dedication to live a balanced, empowered and fulfilling life. As a visionary, Latrina strives to help individual's foster stable success within themselves and beyond.

Email: C2C.Coaching20@Gmail.com

Connect on Facebook:

@C2CCoaching & Consulting

@AuthorLatrinaC

@CoachLatrinaC

@SWOMSocialClub

Kendra McNutt

Co-Author

Kendra has rebuilt her life from a low place, leaving an abusive marriage with 4 small children, and odds stacked against her. She has worked hard to not let the difficulties she's faced break her faith or spirit, but to strengthen them. She has used the strategies she learned to rebuild herself, to help her coaching clients rise above the hardships they are facing too. Her clients learn to love & embrace a life full of passion and joy.

Precious Swain

Co-Author

Who is Precious Swain?

Written by Aja Monique

If I had to describe Precious in one word it would be "survivor".

Despite the many years of trials and pain she survived. Today she is a Minister, founder of New Visions Ministries of Florida, Inc. Author of the "Who Says a Princess Can't Come From the Ghetto?" Series. Collaborator in International Best Seller "Finding Joy in The Journey". A serial entrepreneur-owner of Imprecious Entertainment Services, Founder of Swain Girl Media, and owner of Anointed for Prosperity Business Consulting. She is a wife, a mother, a grandmother, and a walking testimony to the greatness of Yahuwah.

With grace and transparency, she shares her testimony for the benefit and healing of others and the edification of the Father.

Facebook: PreciousSwain.Author

Instagram: AuthorPreciousSwain

Twitter: @imprecious

www.authorprecioussswain.com

Adrienne Horn

Co-Author

Adrienne Horn, a native resident of Miami, Florida, is a young energetic community leader whose primary focus is perfecting literary projects that will positively impact the lives of those who have an enthusiasm for reading.

As a teenager, she developed a love for words and expressed her thoughts through poetry. Although she majored in Pharmacy and Pharmaceutical Sciences at Florida A&M University, she never lost her passion for reading and revision.

Upon graduating, Adrienne embarked on a journey that would allow her to make a positive impact within the literary world. Starting with her poetic circle, she began offering her services to those who were unable to secure an affordable editor for their projects.

Fueled by her desire to make her mark as an independent editor in a corporate-driven industry Adrienne decided to transition her experience by forming her own editing business.

While Adrienne continues to serve the nation in the capacity of a pharmacist, her heart is deeply committed to making the literary world a better place one successfully edited project at a time.

Jakia Cheatham - Myles

Co-Author

Born and raised in Clarksville, TN. Currently residing in Saginaw, MI with her Husband and Daughter. She knew God had a purpose for her life at an young age. Jakia has had to overcome devastating adversity in her life from the time she was a child, but never had to let the challenges obstruct God's calling. She is active in her church. She is also involved in her community and has inspired so many young people to push forward. Author of 4 Books and Creator of Pretty Women Hustle, Pretty and Black Owned and The Church Girl Lifestyle Movement. Her vision and Passion is to proclaim the saving, healing and delivering power of Jesus Christ worldwide. Jakia aims to bridge the gam between business and faith with Pretty Women Hustle.

Tiffany Brewster

Co-Author

Writer, Author, Life Coach & CEO of T.K. London Collection & Silence No More Inc

If you are silent about your pain they will kill you and say you enjoyed it- Zora Neale Hurston.

Alrissa Jenkins

Co-Author

Alrissa Jenkins Sims land is 29 years old. A native to Oxford, MS, she now resides in Crystal Springs, MS. One thing that can be said about Alrissa is that this married, mother of two stays on the move. When she is not helping run her two businesses, Sistas Empire and Sistas Cleaning LLC, alongside her sisters, she loves to read and write. These two hobbies prompted her to attend the University of Southern Mississippi and major in psychology with an emphasis in Child and Family studies. With this degree she was able to develop ways to learn people, so she can better help and inspire others, especially single mothers who must hustle on their own. It also taught her valuable people skills she needed to effectively run her businesses and leave a legacy for her children. She is so excited to be able to collaborate with other inspiring women.

Tia Kennebrew

Co-Author

Born Tia Kennebrew, known as Tia Reesey the ghostwriter. Born and raised in Boston, Massachusetts. Single mother of an awesome kid who has Autism. Tia has spent the past 3 years helping women feed their $5 Jewelry habit with Paparazzi Accessories. Tia enjoys her past time as a freelance writer, blogger and 4th time co-author working towards her own novel. She has a strong passion for writing and has always been very therapeutic as a way to release her emotions.

Kristina Peck

Co-Author

Kristina Peck is a 25-year-old Mother, Nurse, Upcoming Author and Direct Sales Success Trainer. Kristina Joined Pretty Women Hustle Network in the summer of 2020 as Executive Director. Kristina has been dedicated to growing the network of Women and sharing her success trainings with thousands of women. Kristina is currently pursuing a degree in Nursing from Chamberlin University.

Fida Abott

Co-Author

Fida Abbott is an award-winning author. She is from Indonesia and lives in Pennsylvania with her husband and her daughter. She writes in English and Indonesia and has published several books in those both languages. Besides as a Language Instructor for Indonesian serving USAF, recently she holds a new intermittent position as a Language Consultant for Federal Government.

Jessica Kemp

Co-Author

Jessica Kemp is an up and coming children's author with her first book set to release November 2020. She was born and raised in Sault Ste Marie, Ontario before moving to Toronto in 2012. A graduate of the Child and Youth Care program at Ryerson University, she worked many years in childcare before pursuing her dream of becoming a writer. Most recently, she created her brand "The Jessi K Adventures" in which she discusses her upcoming book, as well as her life as mom and wife. Every children's book that Jessica releases will have a portion of the profits going towards a charity/organization.

FB : The Jessi K Adventures

Instagram: @iamjessi.k

Email: jessiKadventures@outlook.com

Erin Montgomery - Jones

Co-Author

Erin Montgomery is a journalism graduate and holds a certificate as a certified book editor. Erin has held positions in PR, Marketing and Communications for the past 15 years. Erin is also the editor and founder of Flourish Magazine written for moms by moms.

Dr. Ketra Davenport - King

Co-Author

Charismatic, Energetic, and Captivating are words that describe the personality of Dr. Ketra. Armed with over 20 years of serving the community, Dr. Davenport-King is an advocate, speaker, mentor, coach, and philanthropist who has radically impacted the lives of believers under the flagship of her ministry.

Dr. Ketra L. Davenport-King, a native of Dallas, Texas, received her Bachelor of Arts and Science in Christian Counseling, Master of Arts in Christian Education, and Master of Business Administration from Dallas Baptist University. She earned her Doctor of Strategic Leadership from Regent University. She has spent much of her life serving people in various capacities. One of her greatest joys is starting Life After Advocacy Group, Inc., in 2004, to help individuals who have been victims of sexual abuse recover and live a healthy life.

Dr. Ketra opened the doors to Rock Dimensional Consulting (formally known as KLD Consulting Services) in 2005. Through RDC, she has spent the past 15 years coaching and training leaders, developing and educating church ministries, hosting leadership seminars, and workshops. Dr. Ketra is known for her innovative and engaging Leadership Seminar name, 'The Leadership ReCourse' designed to reconnect today's leaders back to collaborative

leadership. Dr. Ketra wholeheartedly believes, "when you live in a community, there should be a handprint of your work left behind for future generations." She launched the North Vernon Women's Community Bible Study group in 2015 to bridge the gap and bring together a diverse group of women to improve the family dynamic in underserved communities.

Her latest accomplishment is her new book, Seeing Beyond the Shattered Glass, which is a fictional memoir based on her true-life events. Dr. Ketra is confident that her book will inspire victims of sexual abuse who have suffered in silence to speak their truth

India White

Co-Author

Dr. India White is a motivational speaker, life coach, author, national educational consultant, entrepreneur, and a licensed minister. Audiences learn from her hardships and triumphs in life. As a **former homeless student**, she kicked out of the house on **Christmas Eve** at the age of 16. India is a 3 time graduate from the University of Florida majoring in math and Ed. Leadership, then obtaining her doctorate in Educational Leadership and Administration. She was named **Teacher of the Year** in two counties while publishing 28 books, being an **Assistant Principal, and business owner** of Rising Glory Productions, LLC and the TIM Program, Inc. in Florida. As a **McKnight doctoral fellow**, she aspires to impact education as a transformational leader.

As a **Gates Millennium Scholar and McKnight Doctoral Fellow**, Dr. White has obtained a B.S. in mathematics, an M.Ed in Ed. Leadership and recently received her Ed.D. in Ed. Leadership from the University of Florida. India has used her platform to pay it forward as an educational example while helping to raise multimillions of dollars in s**cholarships** for at-risk students for various organizations including Take Stock in Children, YMCA, and the National Association of Professional Women (NAPW).

India inspires people who want to be known as **overcoming, impactful and dynamic leaders**. **Women leaders in education, business and ministry are attracted to her message and influence**. As a licensed minister of the Apostolic faith, Dr. India White shares her testimony, gifts and her books at women's conferences, tent revivals, radio stations and television shows in Florida, Atlanta, and internationally with Canada, the Caribbean, and Africa.

India is the only one in her family with a college education out of 10 siblings. Her books include "**How to Overcome Obstacles from Your Past", "Success in a Book", "I survived It", and "Employee to Entrepreneur."** India is excited about her new release of her autobiography titled, **"Double for My Trouble!"** She is also excited to be a part of a brand-new book collaborations: one on mental health titled "**It's Not That Easy: Stop Telling Me to Get Over it!**" and another collaboration called **Steppin into Our Territories!** which deals with being in ministry as a warrior for Christ. India desires to help coach many people to a healthy life of success with these book collaborations and her autobiography. India recently released a motivational calendar book titled, "**Flipbook for Overcomers**!" that will help give a motivational boost everyday for every reader. Further, she has now launched her own book collaboration titled, "**The Power of an Overcomer"**, which will be available this summer.

Dr. India White is excited about this book collaboration on pretty women hustle because she is a pretty lady who has had to hustle her entire life, and was excited about the opportunity to share key nuggets with her listeners as to how they can become successful hustlers.

Many people will tell you, "She doesn't just talk the talk; she is a Rockstar."

To Schedule Dr. India White for your next event, visit www.india-white.com or email India.White.123@gmail.com for more information.

Social Media Handles

FB: MsIndiaWhite;

LinkedIn: TheIndiaWhite;

Twitter: Indispeaknteach;

Youtube: Indiawhite123

Instagram: Indi238

Shawntia Lee

Co-Author

Shawntia Lee is President and Founder of College Thriver Education Corporation (CTEC). Her passion drive for excellence, education, diversity, inclusion and self-actualization formed the catalyst which gave birth to CTEC. Shawntia holds a bachelor's degree in Organizational Communications from Kaplan University and a Master's in Leadership and Coaching from Bellevue University. Her innovative and creative leadership skills have helped her to carve out an impressive resume over the years. Shawntia's most recent accomplishment was recognized by two major magazines. She was featured in Sheen and Leading with LEE digital magazine for aspiring, seasoned entrepreneurs, trendsetters, and game changers. Shawntia was specifically recognized for being an advocate; providing representation which paved the way for students of color to access a college education.

Within the context of our rapidly changing world Shawntia's wealth of experience coupled with passion has now morphed into a desire to contribute meaningfully to the learning experience of K-12 and college students. Focused on adding value for a more fun engaging and impactful curriculum, she has created a new learning platform.

College Thriver Platform and Mobile Application is competitive and cost-effective, based on standards within the industry. Training and utilization of this cutting-edge technology-based learning platform is also within the scope of competitive industry timelines.

Shawntia not only believes but acts to help others through networking within and between communities of interest. It was her agile and deft networking skills which positioned her as a much sought-after leader in several industries. Shawntia was trusted by Disney, Siemens, and Lockheed Martin with the responsibility of client partnership. These positions required the ability to thrive in a fast-paced environment while maintaining the highest level of interpersonal communication and relationships. Shawntia's undaunted spirit in the face of challenges and unchartered waters, inspired her to accept a teaching position for a period in Shanghai, China. On every occasion and in all situations, she delivered at above par standards.

Shawntia was instrumental in the strategic planning and implementation of a Business Expo which connected over 500 community members across industries. As a 'Women of Excellence and Leadership' board member Shawntia served to empower business owners to chart their own course in excellence. She assumed the position of board panel member. Shawntia was charged with supporting the organization utilizing her marketing, and networking skills to connect over 300 members engaging them in mutually benefical business opportunities. She also played a pivotal role in selecting a panel for the Women of Excellence and Leadership event. It is now her proven track-record of excellence in creating educational and business solutions that Shwantia has honed and transformed into creating The College Thriver Platform and Mobile Application.

As an innovative, transformational leader in the sphere of business and education Shawntia is no stranger to challenges. Her professional and personal life experiences combined has created a formidable foundation from which her skills and expertise will continue to be launched.

Tiffani Teachey

Co-Author

Tiffani Teachey is a Sr. Mechanical Engineer, Science, Technology, Engineering, Math (STEM) coach/ advocate, professional speaker, bestselling author of What Can I Be? STEM Careers from A to Z, Saving Lives While Fighting for Mine: Stories to Empower Women to Win, and Pretty, Paid & Powerful: 40 Days to Empowering the Hustler Within. As an engineer with more than sixteen years of experience, Tiffani has a passion for inspiring the next generation to engage in STEM careers. She is known for motivating, empowering, and inspiring others to succeed. Tiffani was born and raised in Winston-Salem, North Carolina, enjoys traveling and being a youth mentor. For more about Tiffani, visit her website at www.tiffaniteachey.com, follow her on Instagram and Twitter @tiffaniteachey, or like "Author Tiffani Teachey" on Facebook.

Monica Leakes

Co-Author

Monica Leak is a graduate of Appalachian State University with a Bachelor of Science in Communication Disorders, South Carolina State University with a Master of Arts in Speech-Language Pathology, North Carolina Central University with a Master of Library Science and Master of Divinity from the John Leland Center for Theological Studies. She is the editor and a contributing writer of, *Faith of our Founders 100 Daily Devotionals to Inspire, Encourage and Propel the Finer Woman (2015)* as well as a contributing writer to *Purpose Pushers: The Journey of Discovering and Walking in Your Life's Purpose (2019)* . Her writings have appeared fin the following Lenten devotionals: *The Road to Calvary Surviving a Season of Suffering; Resipiscence, a Lenten Devotional for Dismantling White Supremacy (2018, 2019, 2020 editions)* and the North American Baptist Fellowship, *Journey to Easter.* Her first published work, a collection of poetry telling the stories of those lives lost to police brutality, *No More Hashtags: Remembrance and Reflections* was published in 2018 and its follow-up, *No More Hashtags: Who You Calling?* was published in 2019 . She currently works as a speech-language pathologist in southern Maryland and as a seminary librarian in northern Virginia.

www.ingramcontent.com/pod-product-compliance
Lightning Source LLC
LaVergne TN
LVHW050647100826
845148LV00011B/2013

* 9 7 8 0 5 7 8 8 6 8 7 7 6 *